NEXT STEPS:

Prepare Yourself for Divorce and Hire the Right Lawyer for Your Case

NEXT STEPS:

Prepare Yourself for Divorce and Hire the Right Lawyer for Your Case

An essential book for anyone who is considering a divorce in North Carolina

by

JAMES W. HART, ESQ.

www.jameshartlaw.com

The Hart Law Firm, P.A.
1143-B Executive Circle
Cary, North Carolina 27511
(919) 460-5422

Printed in the United States of America
ISBN: 978-1-7335918-0-5

Hart Media Group
1143-B Executive Circle
Cary, North Carolina 27511

Dedicated to My Mom. I miss you everyday.

Collaborations By

Kristen Wynns, Ph.D.

Dr. Wynns is a child and adolescent psychologist who owns Wynns Family Psychology in Cary, North Carolina. She has a Ph.D. and Master's in Clinical Psychology. At Wynns Family Psychology, Dr. Wynns and her talented team provide therapy for children ages 3 and up, parent coaching, and social skills groups and camps. They also provide psychological and psychoeducational evaluations for ADHD, Autism, Learning Disabilities, and Gifted. Dr. Wynns specializes in high conflict divorce cases by offering co-parenting therapy, reunification therapy, therapy for children of divorce, and a full menu of custodial evaluations. For more information about Dr. Wynns or her practice, visit http://wynnsfamilypsychology.com/.

Alison Sanderson, LPC

Ms. Sanderson runs a counseling practice for individuals and couples in Cary, North Carolina. She is licensed as a professional counselor in both North and South Carolina, and is also a Certified Clinical Mental Health Counselor. For more information about Ms. Sanderson and her practice, visit http://www.sandersoncounseling.com.

Mike Garrett, Ph.D., LPC

Dr. Garrett is a Licensed Professional Counselor and Executive Director of Christian Counseling Associates of Raleigh, with over 35 years of successfully helping individuals, marriages, and families. In his practice, Dr. Garrett offers regularly scheduled counseling appointments, couples intensives, and other forms of marriage-counseling services, all delivered from a Christian point of view. You can learn more about Dr. Garrett and the services he offers at http://christiancounselingofraleigh.com.

Amelia Kelley, Ph.D., LPC

Dr. Kelley is the owner and supervising therapist at Kelley Counseling and Wellness in Cary, North Carolina. Dr. Kelley and her team work with individuals and couples to treat and address substance abuse addictions and other additive behaviors, anxiety, mood disorders, ADHD, adolescent behavioral issues and development, play therapy and childhood stress, trauma recovery, the Gottman method of couple's counseling, and more. For additional information about Dr. Kelley or her practice, visit http://www.kelley-counseling.com.

Table of Contents

Introduction 1

Letter to Prospects (Knowledge is Power!) 3

What This Book Will Teach You 5

Why Did I Write This Book? 7

How This Book is Organized 9

No Legal Advice Here 11

20 Bits of Practical Advice 13

The Basics of Separation and Divorce 17

Section One: The Decision to Move Forward 19

    Ending a Marriage 21

    Separating Your Separation Options 25

    Navigating the Stress of Divorce 29

    Someone Has to Go First 35

Section Two: Legal Separation in North Carolina 43

    Introduction to Legal Separation 45

    12 Steps to Help You Prepare for a Divorce 59

Section Three: Mechanisms for Settlement 77

    Separation Agreements 79

    Divorce Mediation 89

    Collaborative Law 103

Section Four: Understanding the Legal Process.....109

    The Rules of the Game.....111

    How to Get Divorced in North Carolina.....119

    Spousal Support and Alimony.....127

    Dividing Up Your Assets.....133

    Child Custody and Support.....141

    Divorce from Bed and Board.....151

Section Five: Hiring the Right Lawyer.....153

    Do You Even Need a Lawyer?.....155

    How to Hire the Right Divorce Lawyer.....161

    Before You Call to Schedule a Consultation.....169

    Your Next Steps: Final Thoughts.....175

Warning and Disclaimer

This book provides general information and does not constitute specific legal advice.

I am not your lawyer until you and I enter a written agreement for me to be your lawyer. The information and advice that is provided in this book was developed over many years representing individuals in divorce cases. Just because a certain set of facts seems similar to what you are going through does not mean that you should follow the same advice provided in this book.

Every case and situation is different and an attorney only give you proper legal advice after he or she has a full understanding of the facts of your case.

Please use this book for informational purposes only.

Introduction

Thank you for taking the time to read this book. If you are reading this book, you have likely spent a great deal of time working to save your marriage, perhaps using a marriage counselor or therapist, and you have decided that the best option for you and your family is to pursue a legal separation.

For some of you, this is a trial separation, and you have every intention of moving back in with your spouse after a few months. For others of you, this is the beginning of the end of your marriage. Regardless of which camp you fall into, the information in this book will help you prepare yourself for the worst and find and hire the right lawyer for your case.

My name is Jim Hart, and I am licensed to practice law in North Carolina and Florida. I began my own law firm in 2005 because I wanted to change the way people are treated when they need legal help. I am also a firm believer in building solid relationships with everyone that comes into contact with my law practice, whether that person is another attorney, an employee, a marriage counselor or therapist, or, especially, my client. For the past thirteen years, I have sought to change the way people approach divorce by demystifying the process and educating members of the community. My goal for you is to help you navigate this process with a sense of confidence and support the entire way.

I first started handling my own cases as a public defender in Seminole County, Florida, just outside of Orlando. It was there that I gained invaluable courtroom experience and tried numerous jury trials. When I started my own practice, I stopped taking criminal cases and devoted my entire practice to family law and divorce work. Currently, nearly all of my practice is composed of family law cases, including divorce, spousal support and Alimony, Equitable Distribution, and Child Custody and support issues.

I was a child of divorce myself, so I understand firsthand what it is like to be raised in a household by a single parent. I was the oldest of three siblings. That experience is invaluable to my clients as I work with families that are going through the pain and suffering that is a legal separation and divorce.

I have chosen to practice law in a way that is different than most attorneys. I believe in providing excellent, quality information to prospective clients **before** they meet with or hire my office to handle their divorce. Additionally, as I will point out later in this book, not every case requires an attorney! However, I believe that you should have this valuable information now, for free, before you feel pressured to hire the first attorney you meet with.

I thank you again for ordering this book, and for considering my law firm to handle your family law or divorce case. If you have additional questions, please feel free to visit my website at www.JamesHartLaw.com, where you will find a wealth of information and free resources that will help you along this path.

Letter to Prospects (Knowledge is Power!)

Relax. Slow down. Breathe. It is going to be okay. The prospect of going through a legal separation and divorce may seem daunting, but it does not have to be. If you are reading this book, it is because you have tried everything you can to save your marriage, including therapy or counseling, and you are at your wits' end.

You are considering what steps to pursue next, which may include a legal separation or a divorce. You may have already talked with your spouse about a divorce, or possibly have already been served with a lawsuit.

Now is not the time to panic. Life may seem out of control. You have got a lot running through your mind: finances, the kids, wondering if there is anything you can do to save your marriage, and if not, how do you start to wrap your head around the next steps?

I realize that these words may not put you at ease, but I want you to know that after having represented thousands of individuals seeking a divorce over the past thirteen years, one thing has become clear to me: You will get through this. You will come out on the other side happier, stronger, and more excited about the next steps of your life. Starting this process can be difficult and scary, but you do not have to do it all in one day. You can take your time with this part of your journey.

You are trying to figure out what your legal options are. Should you hire a lawyer, and if so, how do you go about deciding whom to hire? Should you talk to your spouse or their attorney about your case? What are you legally entitled to? **I have written this book to answer these questions and more.**

What This Book Will Teach You

This book is intended to help anyone who is thinking about ending their marriage in North Carolina. Separating from your spouse is not an easy decision, and far be it for me to presume that a divorce is the right or wrong decision for you. At The Hart Law Firm, we have worked with thousands of people to help them navigate the minefield that is a legal separation and divorce in North Carolina, and I can tell you that there is no right or wrong answer to the question "Should I leave my spouse?"

This book will teach you about the various rules and statutes you should be aware of if you decide to start the process of ending your marriage. In addition, we will talk about the various methods of resolving your legal case, from simple negotiation all the way to a trial in family court.

Whether you are just starting down the road to a legal separation, or you have already separated and aren't sure what to do next, this book will give you the information that you need to make informed decisions about your case. Ideally, you will read this book *before* you meet with a lawyer.

In these pages, I will show you what steps you need to take to protect yourself in your divorce. If, after reading this book, you decide you need an attorney, this book will provide you with a system for finding the best lawyer for you and your case.

Why Did I Write This Book?

Unfortunately, every day, people decide to end their marriage. They do it for a number of reasons, including lack of communication, differing opinions about how to manage finances, marrying too young, domestic violence, or finding out that their spouse is involved in an adulterous relationship. Sometimes, after many years of marriage, people just grow apart and decide to go their separate ways. I have seen all these scenarios and more. Whatever the case, this book was written for you.

The process of divorce is a difficult and painful one. I often tell my clients that there are two types of divorces: the emotional divorce and the legal divorce. Most people must complete the emotional divorce before they can begin working on the legal divorce. I often encourage my clients to seek counseling (and frequently refer them to professionals whom I know and trust) to help them through their grief or even to help them try to save their marriage before they decide to proceed with a legal separation. Every person is different, and everyone handles their marital breakup in a slightly different way. Some couples part as friends, while others can barely speak to one another, let alone negotiate a divorce settlement with one another.

If you are reading this book, you are considering hiring a lawyer. Perhaps you were blindsided with a lawsuit from your spouse and have nowhere else to turn. At this point, you are overwhelmed with the sheer number of lawyer ads that are in the marketplace—in the yellow pages, on the radio and television, even on the billboards on your drive home from work. These advertisements do not assist you in making any informed choices about whom to hire as your lawyer. I wrote this book to give you the information you need *now*, so that you can feel confident that, when the decision is right, you will be able to take the steps necessary to find the right lawyer for you.

How This Book is Organized

This book is not meant to be read from cover to cover, although you certainly could do that. Instead, I have broken this book into five specific sections, each one covering a different aspect of the divorce process in North Carolina. The first section contains a series of chapters written by some very well respected marriage counselors in the Triangle. They have each graciously agreed to provide their unique perspective on various aspects of ending your marriage.

The second section of the book discusses legal separation. In North Carolina, this is the first major step in moving toward divorce. You must be legally separated from your spouse for at least one year before either of you can file for an Absolute Divorce. Just because you decide to separate does not mean you are destined for divorce—but you cannot obtain a divorce unless you have been separated for a year.

In the third section, we discuss the various mechanisms used to settle your case, including negotiation, mediation, collaborative law, and even filing a lawsuit. If you are not sure how to start the process of conflict resolution with your spouse, this is the section to begin with.

In the fourth section of this book, we will review the legal divorce process in North Carolina. Going into court can be a scary and daunting proposition, and this section is intended to give you some of the information you may need to demystify this process. Will it replace the assistance of a lawyer? No, but it will help.

In the final section of the book, we will discuss the process of hiring a divorce lawyer in North Carolina. This section includes chapters that will help you determine whether or not you even need a lawyer, how to go about hiring the right lawyer, and what to do before you schedule a consultation.

Along the way, if you have any questions or need additional guidance to help you through this process, please feel free to reach out to our firm at (919) 460-5422.

No Legal Advice Here

We are humbled that you have chosen to read this book, and we are truly sorry that you and your spouse are considering legal options to end your marriage.

However, please understand that nothing you find in this book should be construed as legal advice. Every situation is unique, and every case is different. Legal principles may stay the same, but only a lawyer can tell you how those rules will apply to your particular situation.

If you are interested in our legal opinion, we would be happy to meet with you for a no-obligation assessment to review your particular situation and offer advice on how best to proceed given your individual goals and beliefs.

To schedule a meeting with one of our attorneys, please feel free to call our office at (919) 460-5422 or fill out a contact form on our website. Simply visit https://jameshartlaw.com/contact.

20 Bits of Practical Advice

Before we jump into the nuts and bolts of legal separation and divorce in North Carolina, there are a few basic bits of practical advice that you must understand. If you get nothing else out of this book, this information will give you a foundation of practical advice you can use as you navigate this process.

1.   No matter what else you do, consider your needs first. A surefire way to sink your case is to give up the farm before taking care of yourself first. Do not make that mistake.

2.   Do not sign anything without talking to your lawyer first, unless you understand what you are signing and the legal ramifications.

3.   Negotiating a divorce settlement is like a game of chess. Make sure you listen carefully to what your spouse is offering, and try to read between the lines to figure out what they really want.

4.   Think about the worst possible scenario that could come from your divorce. Write that scenario down, as well as how you will overcome it. In no time, you will start to feel better and have a more positive outlook for your case.

5.   You are the only person who gets to live in your shoes. As such, you are the person who will need to live with your decisions about your case and your future.

6. You are best situated to look out for your case. Even the best attorney in the world will not care about your case or your outcome as much as you do.

7. Do not put your children in the middle of your divorce. They are not adults, and you should not discuss your divorce with them. Let your children be children, regardless of what you are feeling or thinking. If you need to talk to someone about your case, call your lawyer or your therapist.

8. Always keep the big picture in mind. Remember that little things that happen today will not matter a year from now.

9. Regardless of how bad things have become between you and your spouse, you will need to co-parent your children forever.

10. The "Law" is the law. It is not always fair or reasonable.

11. Your attorney's job is to help you understand what is happening in your case and advocate on your behalf. But that does not mean you will always get everything you want.

12. Be resourceful. The more information you can gather for your attorney, the better job they can do representing you. You will need information such as tax returns, pension statements, checking account statements, and more to prove your financial situation.

13. Take time to review the laws that will impact your case. If you are seeking Alimony, read the Alimony statute. If you are asking for a division of property, read the Equitable Distribution statute.

14. Turn off Facebook, Instagram, Twitter, and other social networking pages. Unless you rely on these pages for your business, you have no reason to maintain them during your divorce. They will be there when your case is over.

15. Get a new email account with a new password. Use a service such as Lastpass to keep all your passwords secure. Be careful what you do online because a forensic expert can still access your search history even after it has been deleted.

16. If you are seeking custody of your children, never move out of the marital home and leave the children behind. This is a surefire way to lose physical custody. Make sure that whatever you do, your children's needs come first.

17. If you are thinking about moving out with the children, make sure you have talked this through with your lawyer. Making any unilateral decisions about the children, without talking them through with your spouse, can put your chances of gaining primary physical custody at risk.

18. If you are seeking spousal support or may need spousal support, do not ever leave the marital home without a plan of action agreed to in advance between you and your lawyer. In North Carolina, you must be separated before you can file for spousal support, so leaving the house must be done with a firm understanding of the potential consequences.

19. When negotiating a separation agreement, you have a great deal more freedom regarding the terms you will include in the agreement than what a court can do in the courtroom.

20. Your separation and property settlement agreement will resolve all aspects of your divorce in one legal document. **It is imperative that you have a lawyer review your agreement and walk you through its terms** *before* **you sign it!**

The Basics of Separation and Divorce

So you are thinking about divorce. This is an incredibly difficult decision and not one to be taken lightly. Before you start to go down that road, I want to give you a quick overview of the basic process. In subsequent chapters, we will cover more of the details that you need to be aware of.

First, you must understand that divorce is governed by a set of rules, statutes, and procedures that are collectively known as family law. There is no significant difference between going to see a family law attorney or a divorce attorney—they are one and the same. For the remainder of this book, I may refer to either divorce cases or family law cases—there is no discernible difference between the two. In North Carolina, the majority of the family laws are found in Chapter 50 of the North Carolina General Statutes.

Chapter 50 is entitled "Divorce, Alimony, and Child Support, Generally," and can be somewhat misleading because Chapter 50 includes much more than just rules about divorce, Alimony, and Child Support. A few of the main topics governed by Chapter 50 include:

- The legal requirements and procedures to obtain a divorce
- Child Custody

- Child support payments

- Post-separation support and Alimony

- Payment of Attorney's Fees

- Distribution by the court of marital property (i.e., Equitable Distribution)

No two family law cases are the same. Some cases involve only Child Custody and Child Support. Others involve only Post Separation Support or Alimony. Still others deal only with the division of marital property. And others, as you may have guessed, deal with all of these issues. The length of time it will take to resolve your case and the total cost involved will depend in large part on how many of these issues will require resolution with the assistance of a lawyer and/or the court system. North Carolina is unique in that you can resolve any and all of the above issues without ever getting the courts involved. We will talk more about that in the chapter on separation agreements.

Before we jump into these topics, you may have noticed that I have not yet talked about how to actually get divorced—which is the topic you might be the most interested in! In other states, courts will require that you resolve all the issues we have listed prior to granting you a divorce, which means that you must involve the court, at least a little bit, in all aspects of your case. In North Carolina, however, you can get a divorce without resolving anything else in your case. Whether you choose to go this route or not is a decision that is unique to each individual and is not a decision that should be made without discussing it with competent legal counsel first.

SECTION ONE

THE DECISION TO MOVE FORWARD

CHAPTER ONE
Ending a Marriage

By Alison Sanderson

Ending a marriage is a huge life transition and is likely to bring up overwhelming feelings. Like many people, you may be facing feelings of failure or guilt especially when children are involved. You may wonder if you could have done more or what you could have done differently to avoid this situation. You may feel angry or intimidated dealing with a hostile and vengeful spouse who is determined to make you suffer. Know that these feelings are common, and you are not alone. Now more than ever, it is important to have a support system in place to help you through this challenging time. Below are some common issues and strategies when coping with the decision to separate and the transition of divorce.

CAN YOUR MARRIAGE BE SAVED?

If you want to salvage the marriage, you must understand that relationships are co-created, and it will take a true commitment from both of you to do the hard work and change the dynamic of your relationship. A marriage cannot be saved by one person. If one partner has been unfaithful, it still takes both partners to do the work to heal and forgive. If one has a substance abuse problem, both need to do the work to trust and support a sober lifestyle. A therapist trained specifically in couples counseling may be able to help. Seek out a therapist trained in Emotionally-Focused Therapy or the Gottman approach. If substance abuse is involved, seek a couples therapist with training in addiction as well as other group substance abuse programs such as Alcoholics Anonymous or Smart Recovery. Too often, couples will go to marriage counseling for a few sessions and decide it does not work. It likely took years to reach this point, and it can take a significant amount of time to reestablish a secure and healthy bond.

THE DECISION HAS BEEN MADE

If you have already made a final decision to end the marriage, do not beat yourself up about what you could or should have done differently. It is easy to feel guilty for not having the perfect family, particularly when children are involved. You can help your children to understand that this decision is what is best for everyone to move your family forward.

It is normal and natural to be sad; this is a loss, and you will likely grieve, regardless of the situation that brought about the end. However, being guilt-ridden does not solve anything and prevents you and your family from moving forward. Give yourself time and space to go through the grieving process. This will look different for everyone and will likely include bouts of anger, depression, and denial before you finally reach a place of acceptance.

Is Your Spouse Hostile?

Dealing with the stress of a hostile spouse can be toxic to your well-being. If this is the case, it is important to take good care of yourself and to reflect on your ability to set strong boundaries. Do you respond to all of their communication? Do you let yourself get angry or reactive to all of their vindictive slights?

If so, you are giving them exactly what they want. By reacting to their anger, you give away your power. Stay calm and steadfast, and only communicate with them when absolutely necessary. Stand up for yourself, and do not tolerate the violation of implied agreements to respect one another as a person, even in the face of a separation and divorce. If the vengeful spouse feels they can push you around in any way, they will continue to do so. Again, if empowering yourself and setting boundaries is an issue for you, a good therapist can help change your behavior.

Be Careful Around the Kids

Do not disparage your soon-to-be ex-spouse to the children. When emotions are running high and you've been hurt, it can be tempting to trash talk him or her in front of the children. Remember, your children are the product of both of you. Even if your spouse has done something unforgivable, your children can feel as though a part of them is unlovable when they hear hateful words regarding their parent. This is a confusing time for kids, and they often feel that they are partly responsible for the breakup. They need as much responsible, adult behavior as possible from you. If you need to vent, do so with an adult in your support system and out of earshot from your children.

Build a Support System

Surround yourself with a loving and available support system. It is okay to let people know you are going through a difficult time and to ask directly for support if you need it. If you find yourself surrounded by people who are blaming, guilt-tripping, or offering unhelpful and unsolicited advice, you should consider removing them from your circle. This is a time to be extra gentle on yourself. Treat yourself the way you would treat a friend or a loved one going through a painful experience.

Separation and divorce may be one of the most gut-wrenching challenges you ever face. There is no denying that it is hard. However, it will shape you and lead you to the next chapter of your life. Know that you will come out the other side, and you will likely be stronger and wiser for it.

Remember, you do not have to have all the answers and know how it will all unfold. You just need to know the next best step.

CHAPTER TWO
Separating Your Separation Options

By Mike Garrett Ph.D.

Many couples have a binary all-or-nothing approach to marriage and divorce. In other words, they are either all-in or they are all out. Hold your horses! We have worked with thousands of struggling couples, and we know there are other options.

When we do a timeline with a couple to get the 30,000-foot aerial view of their overall history, there are usually several blips on the radar that tell us they have had major ups and downs before. Every couple does have conflict in their relationship, but not every couple does it well. People who have master marriages know how to do it better and faster (and we can teach that), but disaster marriages often take on water quickly as though a massive torpedo has done irreparable damage. The loudspeaker seems to be blaring, "Abandon ship. Abandon ship."

In the case of continual escalated conflict or some form of abuse (which may entail verbal, emotional, spiritual, physical or sexual), we recommend that the couple agree to a therapeutic separation for a reason and a season. It may start with an in-home separation (live in two different parts of the house), but eventually it usually involves one person moving to a different physical location.

The reason for the separation is the hurtful damage inflicted and the inability to peacefully collaborate for healthy change. The season could be for a month or even many months. And we recommend that the focus of this separation time be to aggressively seek counseling for each individual. There has to be some individual work before marriage counseling can be pursued. It takes two healthy individuals in order to make a healthy marriage. We recommend that some form of separation agreement be made during this time. Otherwise the issue of abandonment becomes a liability, especially if there are children.

But the ultimate goal of the separation is to seek individual therapy to work on the main issues that are infecting the marriage. This is not separation for divorce. This is separation to deal with the issues. Many of those couples are able to emerge and reengage with new relationship agreements that lead to a much healthier couple bond. But if the separation is going to be more than a month, we typically recommend a legal separation agreement done with an attorney in order to protect both parties. Couples that resist doing this usually have regrets. Couples who sit down and make this agreement usually are glad in the long run.

If one spouse has already truly abandoned the relationship, then it is time to evaluate if all options for repair and reconciliation have been considered. Counselors, pastors, and best friends (not everyone you know on social media) are usually the right people to pursue during that time. When one partner says, "I'm done," we always like to ask, "Is that your final answer?" If there has been repeated effort at finding and accessing appropriate professional intervention with no cooperation from the partner, then it is definitely time (or even past time) to see your attorney and get a legal separation in place.

We normally recommend taking a collaborative approach, using an attorney to draft the agreement, whenever two partners are willing to sit down and make agreements regarding the therapeutic (or non-therapeutic) separation. If there is little or no agreement on the terms of the separation, then we recommend each spouse find their own attorney since it is going to be a more difficult legal process. Each person will need fair and adequate representation in that case.

This can be a period when the idea of divorce is still kicked down the road while continued therapy is pursued. Separation agreements can always be torn up and discarded if counseling is successful. But for those who are not able to put the pieces of the broken relationship back together, the legal separation and attorney representation will bring some measure of protection, comfort, and reassurance. And you will be glad you did.

CHAPTER THREE

Navigating the Stress of Divorce, a Therapist's Perspective

By Amelia Kelley, Ph.D.

No matter how difficult or frustrating the issues were that led you or your partner to seek out a separation or divorce, the decision is never an easy one. Ending any relationship, even a stressful one, can bring on many difficult emotions that can impact your life, your identity, and your perception of your future. The pain felt can be so intense for some that they report feeling physically ill, and there is good reason as the body does make physiological changes when it goes through heartache or grief. But there is hope, as the body knows how to move past this pain, and you can choose to move through with it. This chapter will explore some of the ways you can care for yourself and come out the other end able to find joy again.

ACCEPTANCE AND THE STAGES OF GRIEF

The end of a marriage can be just as significant a loss as a death of a loved one, because in a way it is the end of the life of your marriage. For this reason, it is important to allow yourself time to grieve with a special focus on self-compassion. Knowing the

James W. Hart, Esq.

stages of grief and how you might expect to navigate through them can be helpful, as it allows for some insight into the unknown. The five stages of grief are as follows:

1. Denial and Isolation

2. Anger

3. Bargaining

4. Depression

5. Acceptance

Most people begin at the first stage of denial and isolation, but how individuals move through the stages from there can vary. Some move through sequentially, while most move back and forth as they learn new things in each stage and may need to revisit a prior stage to further process the change.

For instance, you may enter the stage of bargaining, asking yourself what you could have done differently, and by doing so trigger a hurtful memory that sends you back into the anger stage.

The ultimate goal for every individual is to reach the stage of acceptance, but do not put pressure on yourself to reach this stage instantly. Some individuals may find that they become stuck in the stages of denial or isolation, as a divorce can trigger both new and old emotional pains. It is important not to remain in the stage of denial and isolation for too long. You must try to move forward and push through whatever emotions, thoughts, or reactions to the end of the relationship show up in your life. How gently you handle these emotions can have a lasting effect on your ability to move through the loss.

Some practical ways in which to move forward from the end of a marriage include most forms of expression. For example, some of my clients find that writing a letter (that they do not necessarily intend to share) expressing themselves to the person whom they were in a relationship with can be a helpful way to process and release some of the emotions about the relationship's ending. Others find that simply venting these thoughts and feelings to a trusted person can be equally helpful. It is important to find what works for you to process and express your unfiltered feelings. Now is not the time to censor how you feel. Let yourself feel as upset, sad, lonely, confused, or angry as you need to feel.

If you do not feel like you have the right support network, or maybe those who are supportive do not understand the pain of a divorce, you may find solace in support groups as many do, both online and in person. The presence of others who can understand some of what you are feeling can really help the movement through the isolation phase. Trying to prevent isolation can also help reduce the chance of developing depression, anxiety, or other mental health issues.

GETTING TO KNOW YOURSELF AGAIN

A common positive outcome of divorce for many of the clients I work with is a sense of authenticity and renewal. Allowing yourself to learn and try new things during the time after a divorce can not only serve as a healthy, and at times much-needed distraction from painful feelings, but it can also introduce new areas of self-expansion and discovery. There are many resources accessible for meeting new people and trying new things; one especially excellent resource being online meetup groups. These groups offer people a place to make plans with like-minded people to go out into the world and try things they enjoy.

It may be hard to identify what it is you enjoy at the time of divorce. You may have been so focused on the stress of the relationship that you could have lost sight of what makes you happy. Sometimes it can help to think back to what you enjoyed doing as a child. For instance, if you enjoyed drawing, look for a local art class for adults. If you enjoyed running through fields, perhaps joining a hiking group or making a personal goal to start trekking different places and spaces you have not been would be therapeutic. Doing new things can help with the sense of self-expansion, confidence, and joy that may have been missing toward the end of your marriage.

In addition to going out and trying new things, it is important to take some time for quiet reflection by yourself. Some people find that they need to get to know themselves outside of the relationship on a personal level, almost like getting to know a new person. This can be very hard at times, but it can be exciting, providing you with many messages about who you are, what you need, and where your life will go from here. Sitting in quiet meditation, journaling, or other forms of relaxed alone time can be excellent for your body and mind, which have probably both taken a beating from the process of divorce.

Whether you find the most comfort from being with others, being alone, venting, crying, writing, using coping skills you may have ignored during the stress of the marriage, or all of the above, the most important thing is self-compassion. The more compassionate you are with yourself and the less critical you are of your pain, the more you will be able to process, heal, learn, and move forward. In addition to self-compassion, it is also important to be open to the support from others. You do not have to do this alone; you can ask for help, and you will get through this.

CHAPTER FOUR

Someone Has to Go First (Co-Parenting with a Hostile Spouse)

By Kristen Wynns, Ph.D.

Brenda was resentful and bitter about the judge's decision, which to her seemed blatantly unfair. She had been ordered to pay child support to her ex-husband and she was NOT happy about it. Her ex had been openly hostile towards her in front of their two young girls for many years, even mocking her at public dance recitals and school plays.

What did Brenda do? She delivered the month's child support payment to her ex-husband's house as ordered...all in coins...scattered all over his driveway...with the girls inside his home. While this may seem extreme, after an ugly (or even a "normal") divorce, parents can quickly lose sight of what is best for the kids if they allow themselves to be consumed by negative emotions.

From the moment of separation, you and your spouse begin functioning as co-parents, and how you manage this new reality is vitally important to the well-being of your children.

Research has shown that it is not the divorce *per se*, but rather the amount of conflict associated with the divorce, that negatively effects the children the most. If there is conflict between you and your ex-spouse, your children will be left to deal with an on-going stressful situation at an age when coping skills are still in development and children are not able to process such negativity between parents. Regardless of the actual split of time spent with the children, co-parenting itself is on-going...

WHAT IS CO-PARENTING?

Co-Parenting is when both parents agree to a respectful, cooperative relationship with the sole purpose of parenting their children. Why would a separated/divorced couple ever consider the concept of committed co-parenting?

1. Research shows that children of cooperative divorced parents have higher levels of self-esteem and are, in general, happier and less constrained than children whose parents either don't get along or battle at every opportunity.

2. It's far less stressful on the children as well as the adults.

3. Parents don't get anxious every time they see each other.

4. It facilitates cooperation.

5. It eliminates the shame of fighting and treating each other disrespectfully.

6. Parents can feel better about themselves and the example they set for their children when they treat each other with respect.

Co-parenting may not work in the wake of an abusive relationship or if time is needed to heal from the hurt of divorce before collaborating with the other parent. But, it is priceless to the children when a parent makes every effort to give their children the gift of two parents who love the child more than they dislike each other.

Thus, the time to start lessening the conflict, and build a healthy co-parenting unit is now. Try to move beyond past hurt to forge an amicable co-parenting team for the benefit of your child (and for yourself as well).

Components of a positive shared-parenting relationship include focusing on effective and respectful communication, navigating differences in parenting styles and agree in advance upon difficult topics, engaging in low-conflict joint decision-making, compromising, and portraying yourselves as a united front to the children. Remember that you are your children's role model and the message your behavior sends to your children will teach them the way people should act in this situation.

Co-parenting is an opportunity to teach your children valuable lessons about how to get along with someone even when you disagree with them, how to compromise, and how to maintain positive and healthy relationships even in difficult circumstances. (And yes, these tips apply even if your spouse is not reciprocating the same ideal behaviors).

TOP 10 COMMANDMENTS OF CO-PARENTING:

1) <u>Minimize the child's exposure to fighting</u>. Have your disagreements well out of earshot, and remember that kids are experts at listening in.

2) <u>Resolve conflicts without putting kids in the middle</u>. Don't use your children as messengers or quiz them about your ex-spouse. The less the children feel a part of their parents' battle, the better. Be objective about your children's needs (and don't confuse them with your own) and compromise when the situation warrants. Stick with a conflict until it's resolved; don't let a problem fester and then punish the other parent passive-aggressively or be difficult in unrelated situations.

3) <u>Resist the temptation to let your kids or teens be your support system</u>. Your children may be tempted to act as your confidant and caretaker. Let your friends, adult family members, mental health professionals, etc., be your counselors. Let your children be your children.

4) <u>Remember kids are "half-mom, half-dad."</u> If you engage in making disparaging or derogatory remarks about your ex, your child will take that as a personal insult. Making negative comments about your ex not only hurts your children, but can also damage your bond with your kids.

5) <u>Consistency, consistency, consistency!</u> It's unrealistic to replicate identical discipline, meal, and bedtime routines across both houses. But it does help children and teens when you have some overlap and similarities in these areas. This makes transitions from one household to

another easier, thus minimizing the outbursts from children after visits with the other parent. Respect each other's parenting approaches, and recognize that while consistency is optimal, differences are okay. Children are able to distinguish that while Dad doesn't allow for fast food, and Mom loves the drive though, this translates to differences, not "right versus wrong."

6) Treat the other parent with respect. Be cordial at exchanges and at events for the children. Make eye contact and give a polite greeting. This goes a long way toward easing your relations with your former partner. It also provides a good model for your children; more than we are willing to admit, our children imitate our behavior. Disrespect toward the other parent will be played out by the child. It's important for a child's healthy development to have respect for authority figures, including both parents.

7) Observe appropriate boundaries. When it comes to your kids, it's sometimes difficult to tell yourself what they're doing with the other parent "is none of my business." And if an activity won't harm them physically or psychologically, it probably is none of your business. Recognize it's okay, maybe even good, for children to learn different ways of doing things. It's almost certain that the other parent won't do everything your way.

8) Communicate regularly with the other parent. There's a lot of information to share when co-parenting. Especially when children are small, the other parent needs to know the basics when parenting responsibilities are being transferred. For example, sharing information on meals,

potty training, sleep, and general health is essential for continuity for your children. When children are older, both parents need to know about school activities, homework assignments, sports events and trips out of town. It's recommended that parents get in the habit of sending a brief email or text on exchange days to cover these broad categories of information.

9) <u>Be strict in encouraging and enforcing the visitation and communication schedule.</u> While it may be tempting to allow a whiny or crying child to skip a planned visit or transition to the other parent, this decision may set a precedent that is stressful for both parents in the future. If the child or teen is given the power to choose when he or she goes to the other parent's house or takes a scheduled phone/Face Time visit, this same child or teen may decide he or she doesn't want to see YOU at some point. In addition, what may seem like a desired freedom to choose, may become a burden on the child or teen as he matures.

10) <u>Go First (i.e., "The Golden Rule.")</u> While it may be tempting to lower yourself to the same level of rude and hostile behavior you are observing in your ex, attempt to rise above and set a higher bar. It's hard to continue to heap insults and hatred on someone who consistently responds with grace, civility, and an attitude of cooperation.

Ultimately, your choices and decisions will influence the emotional climate in which your children someday will mature into young adults. Do you want them to remember a toxic sparring match between their parents? Or do you want them to remember they were loved so much their parents put aside emotional wounds and hurt feelings to focus on co-parenting in the healthiest way possible?

SECTION TWO

LEGAL SEPARATION IN NORTH CAROLINA

CHAPTER FIVE
Introduction to Legal Separation

One of the most commonly frequently misunderstood concepts about initiating the divorce process in North Carolina is what exactly constitutes a legal separation. Just because you decide to separate does not mean your marriage is headed for divorce. Many couples need a short separation as a therapeutic tool to cool off, take time to themselves to think, and decide what they want next out of this process.

However, although a separation does not mean you are destined for divorce, you cannot obtain a divorce in North Carolina without first being legally separated for at least one year. The purpose of this section is to explain everything you need to know about legal separation—what it is, how to prove you are separated, what steps you should take to protect yourself legally after you are separated, and more.

WHAT IS A LEGAL SEPARATION?

In North Carolina, a legal separation occurs on the day that a couple physically separates from one another with the intent to live apart permanently. Moving into separate bedrooms is not sufficient. One of you must move out of the marital home and go live somewhere else.

In order to qualify for a divorce in North Carolina, a legal separation for at least one year is necessary. It is not necessary that **both** spouses intended for the separation to become permanent. The intent of only one spouse is sufficient to satisfy the legal requirements in North Carolina to obtain a divorce. However, if one spouse moves out and the understanding by both of you is that the separation is temporary, then the one-year separation period has not started until one of you decides that the separation is permanent.

This is a cause of much confusion for many couples in North Carolina. They may have been separated and working on their marriage for many years, but only recently decided to make their separation permanent and end the marriage. The starting point for the one-year separation period is not the date that they physically separated, but rather is the date that one of them intended to remain physically separated on a permanent basis.

It is important that you understand that only one of you must intend to remain separate on a permanent basis. Even though there is no legal requirement that you tell your spouse you want to move toward a divorce, if you are the spouse who wants the divorce, a good practice is to document the date that you decided to make the separation permanent so that your spouse cannot object to the date of separation when you file for divorce.

If the separation is not mutual, we recommend that you tell your spouse in person and follow up with an email that will have a time stamp showing the date you informed them of your intent to make the separation permanent. Alternatively, many spouses will inform the other of their intent to end the marriage while in a therapy session with the presence of a third-party witness.

PROVING LEGAL SEPARATION

Many people get confused about how to prove they have been legally separated. This is one of the most frequently asked divorce questions that we see in our office. It is important to understand that you **do not** need a separation agreement, nor must you file any paperwork in the court system to prove that you have been separated from your spouse for one year.

After the one-year period has expired, one of you may file for what is called an Absolute Divorce. At that point, you will state under oath that you have been legally separated from your spouse for at least one year and at the time that you separated, you intended that the separation would become permanent. Provided that your spouse does not dispute the separation, this information sufficient. In the rare instance where one spouse makes an appearance in court and contests the date of separation, it may become necessary to offer additional physical evidence to prove the date you separated or show that you informed your spouse that you intended to seek a divorce at least one year prior to filing for divorce.

This evidence can come in the form of a lease agreement for a new apartment, separate utility bills, a change to your driver's license, testimony of witnesses who have visited you at your new residence, or documented evidence showing that you intended to make your separation permanent. A court will look to the "totality of the circumstances" to determine when the legal separation occurred.

Sometimes the date of separation can have a huge impact on other aspects of your case, such as the valuation of property for purposes of Equitable Distribution or the amount or duration of Alimony. If you are in a situation where the date of separation might be contested, you should talk to a divorce lawyer to discuss how best to proceed and map out a legal strategy to put you in the best possible situation for your case.

COMMON MISTAKES

People often make several common mistakes when they decide how and when to initiate a legal separation or file for Absolute Divorce. The first and most common is that people think they can just "make up" the date of separation and then apply for a divorce. The common statement we hear is, "We just separated a couple months ago, but can't we lie and say we separated a year ago?" I am amazed that people continue to ask me this and think that I am going to give them my blessing.

The answer is an emphatic *no*. First and foremost, I would be surprised if you can find a lawyer who would be willing to file that lawsuit for you. Lying to the court is a serious ethical violation and would put the lawyer's law license in jeopardy if caught. Second, even if you were able to handle the divorce on your own and get a judge to grant your divorce, it would require you to lie under oath. Lying under oath constitutes perjury and is a criminal offense in North Carolina and every other state.

Finally, even if you were to lie to get a judge to grant your divorce, your divorce judgment would be void. In other words, you may have a piece of paper that says you are divorced, but you are not actually legally divorced. Your divorce is an invalid divorce because the Court never had jurisdiction to enter the divorce in the first place.

In this case, if your spouse becomes vindictive and decides to make your life a living hell, they could relitigate your entire case all over again at any time in the future. Would you want to live with that your entire life? And if you decided to get remarried, you would be committing bigamy, also a crime in many states.

The bottom line? Do yourself a favor—wait out the year and make sure your divorce is done the right way. This is the only way to make sure you do not have any concerns or issues later down the road.

Can You Live Together and Be Separated?

This is another commonly asked question about legal separation in North Carolina. In some states you are permitted to be legally separated while living in the same house. In North Carolina, you are most certainly not permitted to live in the same residence and be legally separated.

Surprisingly, I have had people tell me during initial appointments that they have been separated for several years. When I ask where their spouse lives, they tell me, "Oh, he/she lives in a separate bedroom down the hall."

Unfortunately, living in separate bedrooms does not qualify as being legally separated in North Carolina. To be legally separated in North Carolina, one of the spouses must physically move out of the residence into a separate residence under a separate roof somewhere else. They must have a new address separate and apart from the marital residence.

There is an exception, however, that I have seen work well if one spouse travels most of the time for work. In these situations, one spouse lives in the marital residence while the other spouse is traveling. When the traveling spouse comes home, the other spouse goes to stay with a friend. When the traveling spouse leaves, the other spouse comes back to the marital home. However, from a purely legal standpoint, we recommend that one spouse move into a separate residence and not return to the marital home.

Another rarely used exception to this would be if the home was partitioned and divided into two separate and distinct living areas with truly separate addresses, such as would be the case if the home was a duplex. In this situation, the married couple would be living under the same roof but would each have their own residence.

WHY A SEPARATION AGREEMENT IS IMPORTANT

North Carolina is one of a handful of states that will allow a divorcing couple to create an agreement (often called a separation agreement or property settlement) that resolves all aspects of their case and keep that agreement completely private.[1] In other words, you do not need to present the separation agreement to a judge to ratify. Some of the issues that can be resolved in a separation agreement include:

- How you will divide all marital property, including financial accounts, retirement funds, and the marital home;

- Determining an amount and duration of Alimony—or provide that no Alimony will be paid at all;

- Establishing a custody schedule and co-parenting plan for the children; and,

- Calculating the amount of Child Support that should be paid.

Many of our clients prefer to keep these very private issues out of the court system and the public eye. A separation agreement can help accomplish this. It is important to understand that a separation agreement is a binding contract, as well as an important legal document. When you sign it, you give up some potentially valuable legal rights. In other words, do *not* sign a separation agreement unless or until you fully understand what is included in the agreement and the impact the agreement will have on your future. If you have any questions about your proposed separation agreement, we highly recommend you seek the help of a divorce lawyer to make sure you understand your rights under the agreement.

At a minimum, you should contact a divorce lawyer to review your draft agreement to ensure that you have not missed

---

[1] For simplicity's sake, in this book I will refer to this agreement as a "separation agreement."

any important issues and that the agreement properly states what you want to happen. There are various legal requirements for a separation agreement to be valid, most importantly that the document be signed and notarized by both spouses. In addition, you must be separated, or your separation must be imminent, for your agreement to be enforceable. In other words, if you are not separated when you execute the agreement, you should separate shortly thereafter.

Is Negotiating a Separation Agreement the Right Choice For You?

Many reasonable people much prefer entering into a legally binding separation agreement where they can negotiate on equal footing with their spouse with full knowledge of their financial situation. You may be one of them. However, this is not always possible. Here are some of the warning signs that indicate when it may be a waste of time to negotiate a legal separation agreement in lieu of going to court:

- Your Spouse is vindictive and hateful;

- Your Spouse has a personality disorder that makes them difficult to deal with and emotionally immature;

- Your Spouse will not share the finances with you;

- Your Spouse has physically or mentally abused you in the past;

- Your Spouse has indicated a willingness to attempt to turn the children against you or denies you access to the children; or,

- You are unable to negotiate on equal footing with your spouse.

All these situations can create a toxic environment in a marital residence. We have seen many cases where reasonable minds would be able to come to an agreement on property, custody of children, and spousal support with minimal cost and emotional expense. However, due to the actions of one spouse acting unreasonable, hateful, or threatening, involving the courts becomes a necessary part of the process.

If you are in a situation where your spouse is acting vindictive, has a mental disorder, is unwilling to share finances with you, or has abused you in the past, then you will likely need a family law attorney to advocate on your behalf. In addition, if your spouse is keeping you from seeing your children, often the only option is to file a Child Custody lawsuit as soon as possible so that you can be allowed access to your children.

Do You Need an Attorney?

Even in situations where both spouses are behaving reasonably, you may need an attorney to help you negotiate a single discrete issue or draft a legal separation agreement for you. Do not attempt to handle this on your own—we have seen way too many DIY separation agreements that leave much room for interpretation and disagreement—not to mention they may not be legally binding in North Carolina.

At a bare minimum, we always recommend that you consult with an attorney at the very outset of your case, before you begin settlement negotiations. This will allow you to get a handle on both what your legal rights and obligations may be before you enter into settlement negotiations with your spouse. Our divorce assessment is perfectly tailored to assist you in this process.

Then, after you have reached an agreement with your spouse, we recommend that our clients come back to us to let us draft the separation agreement for them. In this way, you can make sure that all your bases are covered and that you are legally protected.

However, there are still cases where you find that you are unable to negotiate effectively on your own or that your negotiations stall. If this happens, we are able to step in and use our years of experience in handling family law matters to your benefit. We can let you know whether you or your spouse is being unreasonable and help you finalize your agreement.

DATING DURING SEPARATION

One of the most common questions we get during our initial assessment with a client is whether or not they can start dating after they are legally separated, but before they have entered into a separation agreement. The answer is a definite yes and no. (Brilliant lawyer answer, right?)

Yes, from a purely **legal standpoint**, you may start to date after you are legally separated. However, just because you can does not mean you should. Dating after a separation is a possible sign that you have already emotionally divorced yourself from your spouse.

However, just because you have moved on does not meant that your spouse has. If your spouse is still holding out hope that you will reconcile and is still emotionally invested in your marriage, imagine how devastating it could be to them to find out you are dating. (And trust me, they *will* find out).

Learning that you are dating could be the equivalent of learning that you had an affair, and many jaded spouses will believe you were probably dating your new boyfriend/ girlfriend even before you separated. If this happens, it can lead to all sorts of other legal problems for both you and your new paramour.

We have actually had cases where this has cost a client a substantial amount of money. One husband cost himself almost $90,000 when his wife unexpectedly pulled a settlement offer after seeing him hold hands with another woman in public. As a result, from a purely *practical standpoint*, we typically recommend our clients delay dating until after the ink is dry on their legal separation agreement. There is too much risk involved to not wait a couple of months before starting to date.

WHAT IS A COURT-ORDERED SEPARATION?

In many cases, one spouse will voluntarily leave the marital residence. However, in extreme cases, a judge can order a legal separation. In North Carolina this is called a Divorce from Bed and Board. Many people get confused by this name, because a Divorce from Bed and Board is not a divorce at all, but rather just a judicially recognized legal separation.

To obtain a Divorce from Bed and Board, there must be fault on the part of the spouse against whom the Divorce from

Bed and Board is sought. To obtain a Divorce from Bed and Board, you must prove one of the following:

- Abandonment;

- Malicious turning out-of-doors;

- Adultery;

- Abuse of drugs or alcohol;

- Cruel or barbarous treatment by one spouse to the other; or,

- Indignities to the person of the other spouse to such an extent as to render his or her condition intolerable and his or her life burdensome.

In addition, the innocent spouse must prove that they were a dutiful, supportive, and caring spouse who did nothing wrong toward the other. You should note that actions for Divorce from Bed and Board are rarely granted and are only used in extreme cases. But in the right situation, this is a powerful tool that can be used to force one spouse out of the marital home.

THE LEGAL EFFECT OF SEPARATING

As mentioned previously in this book, a legal separation is important in North Carolina because it is a necessary first step to obtaining a divorce. Unlike other states, if you do not separate in North Carolina, you cannot obtain an Absolute Divorce. In addition, a legal separation is necessary to file claims such as Post Separation Support, Alimony, and Equitable Distribution in Court. And although we strongly encourage our clients to try to resolve their case outside of court through a legally enforceable separation agreement, there are situations where effective negotiations just are not possible.

And this precipitates a common question—should you first negotiate a separation agreement and then move out, or should you move out and then negotiate a separation agreement?

Once again, the answer depends on your situation and how cooperative your spouse is. In highly volatile marriages, where threats are being tossed around like candy at Halloween, we typically counsel our clients to attempt to negotiate a separation agreement before leaving the house. However, in more trusting relationships, we are willing to allow our clients to negotiate an agreement after physical separation has already occurred.

If you are the spouse seeking spousal support, however, your need for support will have a huge impact on this decision. A separation is necessary to file a claim for spousal support in the court system. If you need spousal support but cannot negotiate with your spouse, you must be prepared to file a claim for Post Separation Support as soon as one of you moves out of the residence.

On the other hand, if you are not seeking support, you may want to stay in the house as long as possible so as to force a settlement before you leave. Failing to do so could open you up to a lawsuit as soon as one of you moves out.

CAN YOU RECONCILE AFTER A SEPARATION?

The answer is a surprising yes. Many people need a period of legal separation to take time to work on their own issues so that they can then devote more bandwidth to working on their marriage. Some marriage counselors will even recommend that a married couple take time to themselves to work on the relationship.

As a therapy tool, a legal separation can be very helpful. And yes, a couple can reconcile at any time if they mutually choose to do so. By reconciling, any pending court actions can be withdrawn and hearings canceled. Judges love to hear that couples are attempting to reconcile.

However, a reconciliation can have substantial legal consequences if you have already entered into a separation agreement and have divided marital property as a result of that agreement. Whatever property you have already divided would be considered the separate property of the spouse who received it. Reconciliation can also affect the payment of spousal support and postpone the date that you would otherwise qualify for an Absolute Divorce.

CHAPTER SIX

12 Steps to Help You Prepare for a Divorce

Below are twelve steps you should consider when preparing yourself to begin the divorce process. I have written these steps from the perspective that your spouse does not know that you are considering divorce. It is entirely possible that some of these steps will not apply to you. However, it has been my experience that by following the recommendations below, you can best prepare yourself to manage the process of divorce in a systematic and methodical way. Not only that, but you will save yourself a lot of money in legal fees by taking these steps now, before you go to see a lawyer (except as indicated).

1. FIND THE RIGHT LAWYER.

I wrote this book in large part to help you with this first step. I once read, "You don't need a lawyer to get a divorce, but you need them for the consequences of your divorce." In the next section of this book, "Hiring a Divorce Lawyer," I have addressed simple, no-nonsense ways to determine whether or not you need to hire a divorce lawyer to handle your case, and, if so, how to hire the right lawyer for your case.

First, look for a lawyer that primarily practices divorce and family law. Determine the lawyer's philosophy regarding litigating cases versus settling them. You should look for a lawyer who makes it a priority to attempt to achieve a fair settlement for you outside of court, but who is capable and willing to litigate the case if it becomes necessary to do so.

2. ACCOUNT FOR ALL FAMILY FINANCES.

Next, you will want to gather as much information as you can about your family's financial situation. If you take care of the finances in your household, you may already have a firm grasp on these numbers. On the other hand, you may have no idea what you and your spouse own or owe.

One of the primary functions of the divorce process is to make a division of the assets and debts of the marriage. In order to achieve a fair division, you must know what there is to divide. This is a three-step process:

A.   Determine what you own.

As mentioned above, if you have a good handle on the family finances, then you are a step ahead. If not, now is the time to do your homework. Many of the assets of the marriage will be obvious—the home in which you reside, financial accounts, vehicles, family owned business, etc. Others may not be so obvious, including such things as artwork, bearer bonds, deferred compensation, proceeds from a pending lawsuit, etc. There is also the possibility that your spouse is hiding assets (this is more likely if they are the ones initiating the divorce or if divorce has been discussed previously).

Review all possible assets. Where possible, attempt to gather documentation regarding each asset or account.

Remember to look for or obtain recent appraisals of real estate that you or your spouse own. If your lawyer charges you by the hour, any information that you are able to gather will save you money. If there are documents you are not able to obtain, your lawyer may have to obtain them through the discovery process.

B.   Determine what you owe.

Just as you need to determine what you own, you will also need to determine all the debts you or your spouse have incurred during the marriage (without respect to the name in which they were incurred). Your Equitable Distribution Order or separation agreement will need to address who is responsible for this debt—whether it is in your name, your spouse's name, or joint name.

I recommend that each of my clients obtain a copy of their credit report. This allows you to make sure that you have a firm understanding of all of the debt in your name. It is not unusual for a spouse to have incurred debt in the other spouse's name without their knowledge. If that has happened, you need to know this as soon as possible. There are many ways to obtain a copy of your credit report. You can request a free copy once per year at www.annualcreditreport.com.

In addition, you may want to put a credit "freeze" on your account. You can do this by contacting each of the three major credit bureaus individually. Once you put a freeze on your account, it secures your credit file so that nobody can access it unless you give direct authorization through the credit bureau themselves. Here is the contact information for each credit bureau:

- **Equifax:** Call 800-685-1111 or visit www.freeze.equifax.com.

- **Experian:** Call 888-397-3742 or visit www.experian.com.

- **TransUnion:** Call 888-909-8872 or visit freeze.transunion.com.

Once you see what debt exists, obtain copies of the statements on these accounts to determine the balances. You may also need the statements if your spouse has made large or inappropriate purchases on the cards. In today's internet age, it is relatively easy to sign up for an online account and download several years of account statements.

If you cannot find credit card statements, contact the credit card company directly and request they send them to you. In the event an Equitable Distribution claim is filed, local court rules will require you to produce these statements to your spouse. Therefore, I recommend my clients obtain a minimum of twelve months of statements, and more if possible.

C. Determine income (both yours and your spouse's).

At some point in the negotiations of your family law case, you will need to provide documentation showing your income (if you work outside the home) and the income of your spouse. This is important for a number of reasons, but primarily for child and spousal support.

If you or your spouse is a salaried employee, this will be relatively easy. Obtain a copy of your most recent pay stubs and your income tax returns. If you do not have access to either of these, you can obtain a copy of your Income Tax Returns by requesting them directly from the IRS.[2] An attorney can help you obtain your spouse's paystubs through the discovery process.

If your spouse is self-employed, the job of determining their income becomes much more difficult. This is why discretion about your divorce plans may be important. You may need to discreetly question your spouse (or if they have one, their business partner and spouse) about income. You can attempt to find copies of bank account statements and financial statements of the business.

Another good way to prove income and assets of a self-employed spouse is to obtain a copy of a loan application or net worth statement that they may have submitted to a bank or other lending institution for a loan.

Sometimes it is difficult to prove the actual income of a self-employed spouse. At this point, gather whatever information you can. In the case of a self-employed spouse, your lawyer will likely have to help you by using the discovery process to obtain and analyze additional information - assuming your spouse is unwilling to provide this information voluntarily.

3. PHOTOCOPY ALL FINANCIAL RECORDS.

As you gather all important financial documents, you should make two copies of each or scan them to a thumb drive or dropbox file. One is for you and one is for your lawyer. Keep

---

[2] Complete Form 4506, *Request for Copy of Tax Return* and mail it to the IRS at the address listed in the instructions, along with a $39 fee for each tax year requested. Copies are generally available for returns filed in the current and past 6 years. You can download the form at *www.irs.gov*.

your copy in a divorce notebook or file folder that cannot be found by your spouse. It is important to keep a list of what documents you have, what documents you still need, and which of them you have given to your lawyer.

Each case and each lawyer may require a unique set of documents. In North Carolina, some of the most common documents required under the local rules for Wake County include the following:

- Income tax returns (including business tax returns and K-1s) for at least two years, including W-2s and all schedules and attachments;

- Last three months' pay stubs showing year-to-date income;

- Documents reflecting expenses for current childcare and payments made, healthcare insurance and payments made, and uninsured medical expenses paid (if reimbursement is sought); and,

- Statements for the last six (6) months for any bank account or credit card (including those for a business) in which you or your spouse have an interest.

I also recommend that you collect the following:

- A list of all account names, numbers, contact numbers/ websites of the bank, type of account, and current balance;

- Deeds for all real estate owned by either party individually or jointly (in North Carolina counties, you can obtain these records online); and,

- Statements from the past twelve months from any investment accounts, retirement accounts, pensions, etc., in which you or your spouse have an interest.

4. PREPARE A BUDGET.

The next step in preparing for divorce is to prepare two budgets: one that shows the family financial situation before the divorce filing, and one that is your estimated budget for after separation. This will be important to assist in the negotiation of support payments and ultimately, a separation agreement, between you and your spouse.

Most people do not like to prepare one monthly budget, let alone two of them! However, it is important to know what it currently costs to run your household. This is helpful to show what your "marital standard of living" is. Additionally, you must know what your costs of living will be after you separate. I will go through each below.

Know your current monthly budget.

Knowing the monthly budget is important for the following reasons:

1. In an Alimony case, it is critical to show the marital standard of living and any financial need.

2. It is helpful in assessing specific needs of the children that may not be covered in basic Child Support (e.g., medical needs or private school expenses).

3. It will help you in planning your post-separation/divorce budget.

4.   If your spouse is self-employed and is under-reporting their income, it would be helpful to show that their monthly expenses exceed what they claim their income is. This can show that they are attempting to hide their true income.

5.   A judge may utilize this information to determine temporary support while the case is pending.

You should know this information in order to properly manage your finances whether you are getting a divorce or not!

Make an estimated budget of post-divorce expenses.

This is important for your personal planning and will likely influence your objectives in the divorce negotiations. You need to know your future financial needs in order to evaluate your settlement options or what to ask the judge for in a trial.

There is no doubt that this will take some estimating and guesswork on your part. That is why it is called an estimated budget. This is a work in progress. The point is to give some forethought to what your living expenses will be as you start the next chapter of your life.

Make your monthly budgets.

If you already maintain your checking account records on a software program like Quicken, YNAB (i.e. www.youneedabudget.com), or some other personal finance software, the process will be relatively easy. You can simply print out a monthly budget report. If not, you will need to review your check register and/or your spouse's check register for the past three months. This will reveal the expenses you have both monthly and quarterly (divide the quarterly expenses by three and enter them in the budget as a monthly expense).

You will also want to consider any annual or semi-annual expenses you may have, such as life insurance, homeowner's insurance, car registration fees, etc., and convert those to a monthly figure and enter it in your budget also.

In setting out your budget, try to be as realistic as possible. You should be conservative in your budget (i.e., do not understate the expenses and end up with a budget that does not realistically meet your needs) without grossly overstating the budget (which a judge would frown on should the case go to court). The best advice is to base your budget on the most accurate numbers possible. You may also want to photocopy your monthly bills and receipts to provide proof of your expenses (and provide these to your attorney), should they ever come into question.

5. DOCUMENT AND SAFEGUARD PERSONAL PROPERTY.

Inventory and photograph your household furniture, art, jewelry, and other items of value. Inventory and photograph the contents of any safe deposit box or safe your family may own. Also, photocopy any important documents in the safe or safe deposit box (if you did not already do so when collecting the financial records).

Unfortunately, these documents and property often "disappear" once the divorce process starts—so get your proof in place now. Additionally, you may want to consider safeguarding any items of particular value (either monetary or sentimental) which are small in size. I am referring primarily to things like the jewelry your mother passed down to you, your father's fountain pen, your high school yearbook, your childhood photo albums, etc. Your spouse may not share your desire to divorce with dignity. Better to safeguard those items that are particularly difficult to replace.

I am NOT suggesting that you empty your house of all its contents. That is a sure way to escalate the divorce and to guarantee that you will not have a civilized divorce. Things like DVD players, smartphones, and laptops can be replaced. Just document those on your inventory and photograph them for proof in the event it is ever needed.

A quick note about laptops: I recommend purchasing an external hard drive and making a backup of your home computers. If your spouse takes the computer and all the information on it, it is easier to recover this information (financial data, family pictures, music, etc.) through a backup than through litigation.

6. ESTABLISH YOUR OWN CREDIT (IF NECESSARY).

If you do not have your own credit history, you should begin the process of establishing it now. Obtain a gas card and a credit card. You will need to have your own credit established after the divorce. The sooner you begin this process the better. Do not wait until after the divorce. You can and should start this process immediately.

Once you have obtained the accounts, you can improve your credit by using the cards and then paying them off each month. At this point, **it is important that you use these cards only to the degree that you can pay them off each month. Your**

goal is to establish a favorable credit history, not to run up a bunch of debt that will complicate your divorce.

7. ASSESS THE FINANCIAL ACCOUNTS.

If you have already completed steps two and three, you already know your existing accounts and balances. You now need to decide what to do with them.

It is an unfortunate reality that one of the first things some spouses do when they learn or decide that a divorce is imminent is to empty out or transfer the financial accounts. This is typically done after receiving particularly bad advice from an adversarial lawyer or a well-meaning but poorly-informed friend.

In a perfect world, neither party would touch the financial accounts except to pay normal household bills until after the divorce is over. However, if this were a perfect world, you would not be reading this book, and I would be in another line of work because divorce lawyers would be unnecessary!

I do not recommend that you clean out the accounts. Doing so will immediately escalate the conflict and stress of the separation and divorce. It also will not be well received by the Court, and could subject you to sanctions, including contempt of court and possible incarceration.

However, you do want to be protected from your spouse cleaning out your accounts. If you have a reasonable fear that your spouse will raid the accounts, the only solution is to remove one half of the funds from any joint accounts and put that money into a new account in your own name. Do not hide, dispose of, or waste the money. Document carefully where every penny is spent because you will likely need to make an accounting of it later.

Additionally, you should not do this for the regular checking account out of which the household expenses are paid unless there is a substantial balance in the account over and above the amount needed for paying the current month's bills. You do not want to take action that would cause checks to bounce.

I do not make this as a blanket suggestion. If the money can be kept there and neither party will remove it, this is preferred. Another option for certain types of accounts is to file a temporary restraining order and freeze the account. Clearly, that is only practical for accounts that are not regularly needed to pay bills and regular expenses.

Before you decide how to handle your financial accounts, consult with a lawyer. If they suggest you take all of the money out without a good reason, I would seriously consider whether that lawyer shares your desire for a civilized divorce.

8. ADDRESS CREDIT CARDS AND OTHER LINES OF CREDIT

If a divorce is imminent, you do not want to be liable on any accounts on which your spouse has charging privileges. It is not unheard of for a spouse, angered upon learning of a divorce, to run up charges on all the credit cards. Likewise, some lawyers may advise their clients to take out cash advances on joint cards to provide a cushion while the divorce is pending or to charge a large amount in lawyer's fees to joint cards.

You will want to consider canceling such joint accounts or at least reducing the spending limits. Be aware that this may have an adverse effect on your credit score. However, this temporary inconvenience will be more than offset by the peace of mind you will have by knowing that your spouse cannot run up credit in your name. If your spouse is an authorized user on charge cards in your name, see what steps the credit card companies require to remove them as an authorized user, and do so as quickly as possible.

With some cards, you may simply deactivate your spouse's card online or through an app on your smartphone. We highly recommend you consider doing this if the option is available to you.

Also consider home equity lines of credit. You may need to consider whether you should close them or restrict access pending the resolution of the divorce. Whatever you do, you must seriously consider how to manage the use and availability of credit both before and during your separation, and discuss it with your lawyer before making a final decision.

9. AVOID TAKING ON ADDITIONAL DEBT.

This preparation step goes hand-in-hand with assessing how to handle credit accounts, but deserves to be mentioned separately. While you are in the middle of a divorce, or even if you are just starting to think about separating, you want to be conservative with your finances. Now is not the time to put in a pool, buy a new car, or buy new furniture. You want to simplify your financial situation, not make it more complex.

Before your divorce can be fully resolved, you and your spouse (or the court if you have a trial) will need to allocate who will be responsible for which debts. Generally speaking, the less complex your debt situation is, the easier this task will be.

Please remember that this is only general information. Your own specific situation may require you to deviate from this advice. For example, there are times when you may have to get an automobile and it would be better for you to make this purchase before the divorce is final because you will not have sufficient credit on your own to obtain a loan after the divorce. Once again, this is another reason why you will need the advice of a good attorney, which is why I wrote this book in the first place!

10. WHO MOVES?

One of the most common questions I am asked by my clients is whether they should move out of the house or if they should ask their spouse to move. In North Carolina, if you want a divorce, you must separate from your spouse for at least one calendar year.

Practically speaking, this poses a number of problems—not the least of which is how to pay for two households on the income that is accustomed to supporting one household. A number of factors should play a role in determining who should move out:

- Does either spouse have a non-marital claim to the marital home? In other words, did one spouse own the house prior to the marriage? If so, that is likely the spouse that will stay in the home.

- Are children involved? It is never easy to uproot children, especially once they have started school. If you and your spouse cannot agree on a fair custody arrangement, both of you may refuse to leave until an agreement can be worked out between the two of you. You may need an attorney to help you to draft this agreement.

- Do you have a dual-income or a single-income household?

- Do you or your spouse have family or close friends that one of you can stay with temporarily?

Unfortunately, there is no way to get around this legal requirement. You must separate, and you must stay separated for at least one year. Things are stressful. They will likely get worse before they get better.

Moving out of the house can have dramatic effects on your case. Do not do it without discussing the move with your lawyer and giving it a great deal of thought.

One caveat here: If domestic violence is an issue, then all of this is moot. You will need to take whatever steps are necessary to protect yourself. Remember to keep your lawyer informed about what is happening in your situation. If the Court finds that there are grounds to issue a permanent injunction against domestic violence, your spouse may be removed from the marital home.

11. KEEP A DIARY OF EVENTS.

It is important to document all major events that occur during the course of your divorce and separation. Your lawyer may want your help in reconstructing a chronology (a list in order by date) of the major events that led to your separation and, ultimately, to the filing of the divorce.

Additionally, you should begin keeping careful records of new events and incidents as they occur. Simply note the date, what happened, and any witnesses that may have observed it. In the unfortunate event that your case drags on, events will begin running together and your memory may fail you. This will become a resource that you can refer back to, review while meeting with your therapist, and use to remind yourself why you have decided to pursue a legal separation in the first place.

Resource Tip: Consider using an online journal such as Penzu or Day One (https://penzu.com or https://dayoneapp.com) to keep track of daily events. You can quickly export your entries to PDF and send them to your lawyer if needed. We recommend these apps over a handwritten diary because they are easier for lawyers to read and frequently include date stamps showing the times that the entries were made.

Another caveat. You should discuss this recommendation with your lawyer before implementing it. Some lawyers may not want you to have an ongoing record like this because it could be obtained by the other lawyer during the discovery phase of your case. Or they may want you to take steps to protect it from being discoverable by the opposing lawyer. These are technical legal issues beyond the scope of this book. Just make a note to talk over this recommendation with your lawyer first.

12. BE GOOD!

Here is the principle: you are about to be put under a microscope. You have purchased and are now reading this book, so I assume you may be facing a divorce and want this unpleasant process to be finished as quickly and as amicably as possible. Unfortunately, that is not always possible. For whatever reason, your spouse may not share your wish for an amicable divorce. They may be influenced by others (lawyers, friends, their own personal bias, etc.) who will convince them that what you are offering is not fair.

Although over 95% of divorce cases settle outside of Court, there is always a chance that your case will end up going to trial regardless of how diligent you and your lawyer are about attempting to resolve the case fairly and quickly. That being said, you should not put ammunition in the gun for your spouse to use against you.

That means no dating, no drug use, and no partying. If custody may be an issue, it means making the children your number one priority (they should be that anyway, right?) Even things that are perfectly legal and harmless any other time can be twisted to look suspicious (or worse) in the hands of your spouse's lawyer.

Suppose, for example, that you go for dinner and drinks with co-workers to celebrate a fellow employee's birthday. Harmless enough, right? In a custody case, however, this situation could lead to such questions being asked: While you chose to go out drinking with your friends, your spouse was at home taking care of the children, correct? Are you having a romantic relationship with Joe/Jane who was also at the party? How many drinks did you have that night? This is something you routinely did during the marriage, is not it (i.e., choosing social events over your family)? You drove home that night under the influence of alcohol, didn't you? You get the idea.

One more example: I once conducted a mediation where I expected we would reach a quick settlement. The opposing spouse had already prepared an offer to my client, and we were prepared to accept it. My client had hemmed and hawed over whether he should take it, even though his wife was being more than fair, as she was offering one-half of the equity in a non-marital property that she alone owned. When we arrived at the mediation, this offer was no longer on the table. My client was upset, and I did not understand what had changed about the case. I later learned that, unbeknownst to my client, his wife had seen him holding hands in public with another woman, causing her to take back her offer. This one moment of indiscretion cost my client almost $90,000. (This case was in Florida. In North Carolina, this event could lead to a mandatory Alimony payment, or tort action for Alienation of Affection or Criminal Conversation).

During your divorce, you will want to spend quality time with your kids, go to work, stay around the house, exercise, and attend to your spiritual life. *Be above reproach*. Be Good.

SECTION THREE

MECHANISMS FOR SETTLEMENT

CHAPTER SEVEN
Separation Agreements

A separation agreement is one of the most common ways to resolve the legal aspects of your divorce, particularly in North Carolina. The reason that separation agreements are so prevalent in our state is that residents of North Carolina must be separated for at least one year before they can file for divorce.

As a result, many people find themselves in legal limbo, living separately and apart from their spouse while waiting to file for divorce, but at the same time still considered married under the law.

In order to clarify their rights and obligations as a spouse, many couples will negotiate and enter into a legal separation agreement that will resolve all matters of property, support, custody and much more related to their legal separation.

The purpose of this article is to give you an overview of what a separation agreement is and is not, explain why you should or should not consider negotiating one, and answer some other frequently asked questions that we see from clients who are considering entering into a legal separation agreement in North Carolina.

What is a Separation Agreement?

A separation agreement is a private contract that is negotiated between a married couple that is considering a separation and, potentially, a divorce. A separation agreement frequently contains two separate agreements, one that provides for spousal support (also called Alimony or Post Separation Support), and the other which divides marital property. When you enter into a separation agreement in North Carolina, it is frequently called a "separation agreement and property settlement." The legal reasons for this are complicated and beyond the scope of this chapter.

A separation agreement is an **important legal document** that spells out your rights and responsibilities in the event you decide to separate from your spouse. It will outline how your property is divided, how much alimony is paid and for how long, what your custody schedule for the children will be, how much child support will be paid, and much more.

The separation agreement will also allow you and your spouse to waive any marital rights you would otherwise have, live free from interference of each other, and ensure that neither you nor your spouse can file a lawsuit in court for any issues that are resolved in the separation agreement.

When Can You Enter a separation agreement?

You can enter into a separation agreement at any time, whether you are separated or not. However, the support provisions of a separation agreement (i.e., alimony or post separation support) are contingent on a true physical separation from your spouse.

In the event that neither one of you moves out, those provisions become invalid.

We have worked with clients who want to enter into a separation agreement before they physically separate, as well as with others who have been separated for many months prior to entering into an agreement.

THE BENEFITS OF A SEPARATION AGREEMENT

Many people grossly underestimate the importance of negotiating a separation agreement outside of court. As mentioned before, the purpose of this agreement is to settle all issues related to your marriage without the need to file a lawsuit and have a judge decide. By voluntarily agreeing to resolve these issues out of court, you can substantially reduce the overall legal cost related to your divorce and eliminate much of the stress that comes with going to court.

Litigating things like Alimony, Equitable Distribution, and Child Custody can easily run into the tens of thousands of dollars. Hiring a lawyer to draft an uncontested separation agreement, however, should only cost a couple thousand dollars. In addition, an uncontested separation agreement gives you much more control over the process than giving these issues to a judge to decide.

Typically, only a small percentage of cases (5% or less) make their way to a final trial or hearing in front of a judge. And even in those cases, many will resolve on the day of the hearing as one or both parties start to become nervous about the prospect of letting a man or woman in a black robe decide their fate. If you can shortcut this entire process by resolving your case out of court, you will have much more control over how your case is handled.

Finally, we should point out that the financial cost of litigation is only one part of the equation. The emotional cost of litigating a contentious divorce can rip at families for years, especially where there are small children involved. You can avoid this heartache and stress by agreeing to negotiate and enter into a separation agreement outside of court.

Here are some of the most important benefits to negotiating a separation agreement out of court:

Control – With a separation agreement, you have complete control over the agreement. You can negotiate any settlement you want and can agree to things in a separation agreement that a judge would never put into a court order.

Privacy – A separation agreement and property settlement often contains very sensitive financial information. Most people do not want this information to become public—but if you decide to go to court, that is what will happen. With a separation agreement, you can keep your affairs private and away from snooping eyes.

Cost – A family law trial is incredibly expensive, typically running into the tens of thousands of dollars. An uncontested separation agreement, by contrast, is much less expensive.

Time – Aside from being expensive, a family law trial can also take a long time to be heard by a judge. Some clients are separated and divorced for several years before their case ever comes before a judge. A separation agreement can typically be negotiated in a matter of a few months.

Do You Even Need a separation agreement?

Not every divorcing couple needs a separation agreement. If you did not own property together (such as a house), have no children, and neither of you is dependent on the other, then a separation agreement may not be necessary. However, even in those situations, you may want a simple separation agreement to clearly terminate your legal rights and obligations as a married couple.

For example, you may want to make sure your spouse has no rights to your estate should you die before you are divorced. Or you may want to ensure that both of you have waived any right to Alimony or Post Separation Support. Most importantly, you may want to make your date of separation clear in the event that either of you decide to proceed with a divorce after you have been separated for a year. To do those things you will need a separation agreement.

Do You Need an Attorney?

Probably. In all honesty, it depends on how complicated your personal situation is and the number of assets you will need to divide. Family law is extremely complicated. Many legal issues can arise in negotiating and drafting a separation agreement that can become problematic later on if you do not have a lawyer review your agreement now.

Remember, a separation agreement is a legally binding contract. While it may seem expensive at the time, hiring a lawyer to review your agreement for you could save you thousands of dollars in the future if things go south.

Whether you decide to have an attorney draft your separation agreement or not, we still highly recommend that you have a lawyer review it before you sign it.

WHAT CAN A SEPARATION AGREEMENT DO?

A separation agreement can provide you with a legally enforceable contract that resolves all the issues related to your marriage. It also allows you to avoid getting involved in in a costly and contentious court battle. Some of the issues which can be resolved in a separation agreement include:

Custody – If you have minor children, you can include a visitation schedule in your separation agreement, as well as determine who will have physical and legal custody of your children. You may also determine an appropriate holiday visitation schedule.

Child Support – In North Carolina, Child Support is typically calculated according to the income of the parents, the number of children, the percentage of overnights with each parent, as well as other variables. You and your spouse may agree to follow the North Carolina Child Support Guidelines, or you may agree to a different arrangement. Regardless, you can include this information in your separation agreement.

Property Settlement – One of the largest and most complicated areas of a separation agreement is the section that divides up your financial assets (including bank and retirement accounts), real estate assets, vehicles, and other personal property. This is a section where many people make mistakes, so it is wise to have an attorney review your property settlement before you sign your agreement.

Alimony and Post Separation Support – In this section you may outline how much Alimony will be paid and for how long. You can also address such issues as who will pay for health insurance and unreimbursed medical expenses, and for how long.

Other Important Provisions – In other sections of the separation agreement you can contractually terminate many marital rights you would otherwise have, as well as include special language that will allow you and your spouse to buy and sell real estate as if you were not married. In essence, you can divorce each other contractually until you have been separated for one year and are ready to file for an Absolute Divorce.

How Do You Enforce a separation agreement?

A separation agreement is a legal contract that can only be enforced in the same ways that any other contract can be enforced. Typically, enforcement means filing a breach of contract lawsuit in civil district court.

Although it is rare to do so, some people will have their agreement "incorporated" into their divorce judgment, making everything in their separation agreement part of a court order. By doing this, your separation agreement becomes enforceable through the contempt powers of the court. This is a much more serious enforcement option, as the offending party could be incarcerated for failure to adhere to the agreement.

Sometimes, people will pull out the support and custody provisions of their separation agreement and place those sections into a "consent order" that is then filed with the court. In this way, if the person who is supposed to pay support stops doing so, they could be held in contempt of court. However, the property settlement provisions of the separation agreement would remain in a private contract.

There are positives and negatives to having your agreement be enforceable as either a contract or a court order, and you should speak to an attorney to determine which option is best for you.

WILL YOU STILL HAVE TO GO TO COURT?

If you and your spouse agree to enter into a separation agreement, you typically will not need to go to court. The entire point of negotiating and entering into a separation agreement is that you can keep your affairs private and outside of the public eye.

People with significant marital estates or alimony obligations may not want this information becoming public in a court proceeding. Having a private separation agreement is a perfect solution in this scenario.

However, if your agreement breaks down or you or your spouse violate the terms of the separation agreement, then you may still have to file a lawsuit to enforce your agreement.

Although you are not guaranteed to be able to stay out of court, most people, after signing a separation agreement, will not need to go to court.

CAN YOU MODIFY YOUR SEPARATION AGREEMENT?

It depends on what the agreement says. In most situations, separation agreements are not modifiable without the written consent of both parties.

However, some people will insert modification provisions in their agreement. Most often, the modification will concern the payment of alimony. People who are paying alimony want to know whether their payment can change or terminate if the dependent spouse gets a job or if their income decreases.

However, if you make your alimony agreement modifiable, it also means that the dependent spouse can ask for an increase or to extend the term of the alimony. For these reasons, many couples elect to receive a certain amount of alimony for a certain period of time and make the payment non-modifiable.

Incidentally, if alimony is placed in a court order it can always be modified if there is a "substantial change in circumstances."

CHAPTER EIGHT
Divorce Mediation

Divorce mediation is one of the most common and effective ways to resolve both the financial and custodial aspects of your case if you are going through a separation and divorce in North Carolina. However, divorce mediation is also one of the most frequently misunderstood methods to resolve your case. It is unfortunate, but most people just don't understand what mediation is.

In this chapter we are going to give you a brief overview of what mediation is, what you can expect if you are thinking about using mediation in your case, and talk about the benefits and limits of divorce mediation. At the end of this chapter we will give you some tips for how to make the most from your mediation session, and then end with a discussion of how long mediation takes, the cost associated with mediation, and whether or not you need a lawyer to represent you in your mediation.

WHAT IS DIVORCE MEDIATION?

A lot of people are confused about what mediation is and how it works. First and foremost, you need to understand that mediation is a voluntary process. That means that even though you may be court ordered to attend a mediation session, nobody, including the mediator, is going to force you to make a decision or agree to a settlement that you aren't comfortable with.

The most frequently mediated issues in North Carolina include child custody, equitable distribution, and support payments (such as child support, post separation support and alimony).

Mediation in North Carolina can be either court-ordered or voluntary. A mediation is conducted with the help of a neutral third party, called a mediator. Mediators are frequently other divorce lawyers, but they do not need to be. They could also be mental health professionals, clergy, or other non-lawyer professionals who are trained and certified by the State to provide mediation services.

During the mediation, both you and your spouse will meet individually with the mediator, typically at the mediator's office or in a courthouse, in an effort to resolve all or certain portions of your divorce case.

The divorce mediator's role is to quickly and efficiently assist you and your spouse in identifying the issues that need to be resolved in your case, and then help you resolve those issues with as little conflict and animosity as possible. Mediation can occur during the course of a single day or over the course of many mediation sessions lasting multiple days.

Mediation is also a confidential process. In addition to being unable to you to agree to a resolution that you do not agree with, and the mediator can never testify about what occurred during your mediation session.

If you reach an agreement, the mediator will prepare a memorandum that outlines the issues that were resolved during the mediation. Both parties will sign this document. Because mediators are not permitted to provide legal advice, you can then take this memorandum to your lawyer to draft a legally binding separation agreement, or in the case of a court-ordered mediation, a consent order for execution by the judge.

You can resolve all issues in your mediation, some of the issues, or none of the issues in your case. In the event you make a good faith effort to resolve your case but cannot do so, the mediator will declare an impasse.

There are two main benefits to mediation. First, the process is much less expensive than filing a lawsuit or continuing to litigate a case that was previously filed. Second, you can control the process and the resolution—something you lose when you go in front of a judge. We will go into greater detail on the many other benefits of mediation later in this chapter.

In mediation, you are typically responsible for your own Attorney's Fees (however, this is an issue that can be negotiated), as well as half of the mediator's fees. Again, we will talk more about the cost of a mediation in just a bit.

You can bring your lawyer to mediation, but in some cases (such as court ordered custody mediation), lawyers are not permitted. In the right situation, divorce mediation is an efficient and cost-effective way to resolve your divorce in North Carolina.

WHAT HAPPENS IN A DIVORCE MEDIATION?

Mediation is much different than going to court. If you go to court for a hearing, you will present your evidence and argue your case to the judge. At the end of the hearing, the judge will make a decision that you will be bound to follow.

The way a mediation works in Wake County, North Carolina may be slightly different than what you would experience in other counties and states across the country. When you first arrive at the mediator's office, you will be escorted into a conference room which will be your "home" for as long as the mediation lasts. Assuming you have hired a lawyer, they will meet you at the mediator's office.

In Wake County, a mediation will typically start around 9:30 am and, in the majority of cases, will last the entire day. We frequently tell our clients not to schedule anything else on the day of mediation, and to make sure that they have childcare arrangements for the kids.

First the mediator will meet with both you and your spouse individually. They will give you a brief introduction to their role as the mediator and explain the mediation process to you. They will explain some of the rules of mediation, and will have you sign some paperwork allowing them to serve as your mediator. Because the mediations take so long, the mediator will frequently order lunch for all of the parties.

Early on in the day, the mediator will spend a lot of time with both you and your spouse to get a feel for who you are and what you are looking to accomplish during the mediation. Later in the day, as the contested issues become more clear, the mediator will move between rooms much more quickly.

As your lawyer, we will sometimes meet with the other lawyer and the mediator alone to give them a quick rundown of the facts of the case and the legal issues involved, or even to address some roadblocks that sometimes arise during the course of the day. The remainder of the time, we will be in the room with you to explain your options, answer any questions you have, and work on preparing various settlement scenarios.

In some mediations, you will start the process off by meeting with the mediator and your spouse in the same room. In other mediations, you will start in a separate room and will never see your spouse at all. Instead, the mediator will bring settlement offers back and forth from your room to the room your spouse is working in.

WHAT ARE THE BENEFITS OF DIVORCE MEDIATION?

Divorce mediation is a form of alternative dispute resolution. This means it is an alternative method to resolve your case that does not involve a judge and a courtroom. Mediation is one of the most common and popular methods of alternative dispute resolution for a number of reasons:

1. **It is easy to implement**. Judges can order people to mediate their case right there in the courtroom and do so with great frequency.

2. **It is built into the judicial process**. If you want to go to court to resolve your family law case, you will frequently be court ordered to mediate your case before a judge will hear your matter.

3. **It is cost-effective**. You can accomplish more in one day of mediation than often can be accomplished in months of litigating a case.

4. **It is private**. All of your negotiations, as well as your final agreement, can be kept private and out of the public eye.

5. **You retain control**. You (not a judge) will ultimately decide whether or not to settle your case, and under what terms.

However, even though divorce mediation is so prevalent and popular, many people do not fully understand what is can and can't do for your case.

WHAT ARE THE LIMITS TO DIVORCE MEDIATION?

There are a number of limits to the divorce mediation process. Here are just a few:

1. Nobody can force you to mediate your case.

2. Nobody can force you to resolve your case.

3. The mediator cannot give you legal advice.

4. The mediator cannot draft a legal contract (or separation agreement) for you.

5. Not all mediations are successful.

Let's review these one at a time.

CAN ANYONE FORCE ME TO MEDIATE MY CASE?

No. Nobody can force you to mediate your case. But the Courts can force you to be appear at mediation and put forth an effort. The mediator has an obligation to try to move your case towards settlement. But if they realize that you have no intention of settling your case in mediation, then the mediator will declare an "impasse" and send back a notification to the court that mediation was attempted and was unsuccessful.

CAN ANYONE FORCE ME TO RESOLVE MY CASE?

As mentioned above, nobody can force you to do anything in mediation. However, the mediator is likely to take time to explain the benefits of mediation and will try to persuade you to engage with the process.

Even if you have spent an entire day working towards a settlement and you have resolved nearly everything about your case with the exception of one small issue, nobody, including the mediator, will force you to sign a settlement if you aren't happy with all of the terms. That means that you can still walk away from a full day of mediation without an agreement if you so choose.

CAN THE MEDIATOR GIVE ME LEGAL ADVICE?

The mediator serves as a neutral third party. That means that they cannot give you advice about whether the deal you have negotiated is a good one or a bad one. They can't give you legal recommendations. That is what a divorce lawyer is for, and why many people bring a lawyer with them to their mediation. The lawyer is there to explain the process to the client and help them decide what to do. These are things the divorce mediator cannot do.

CAN THE MEDIATOR DRAFT MY SEPARATION AGREEMENT?

Unfortunately, no. The mediator's role is to help you and your spouse reach an agreement on all possible issue. They cannot serve as mediator AND lawyer. This is yet another reason why many people will choose to bring their own lawyer with them to the mediation. The lawyer can work to draft a separation agreement throughout the course of the mediation so that at the end of the day, in some cases, you will have a valid and binding separation agreement completed and finished.

DO ALL DIVORCE MEDIATIONS END SUCCESSFULLY?

The overwhelming majority of divorce mediations will end in success (typically 80-90%), but there are still a few that will end with an impasse, no matter how hard you try to work towards a settlement. This happens for a variety of reasons, and it isn't always predictable which cases will settle and which will not.

5 KEYS TO A SUCCESSFUL DIVORCE MEDIATION IN NORTH CAROLINA

There are a number of things that you can do to insure that the time and effort you put into mediating your case will result in a final agreement. This is one of the main questions we get - "can you guarantee that if we spend all this time (and money) preparing for and mediating our case, will it get resolved?"

And the answer is clearly no, we cannot guarantee any particular outcome. But there are things that can be done to increase the likelihood that your divorce mediation will end in success.

#1 Be Prepared for the Mediation

One of the best ways to insure success in your mediation is to be prepared. This is where the best divorce lawyers really earn their money. Mediation is somewhat of an art and not a science. If you want to have a successful mediation, you need to have done your homework before you start the mediation.

This means that your lawyer should have requested and received sufficient information to allow you to settle your case. If one of the issues you want to settle is child support, but your lawyer has not received the proper information about your spouse's income or the cost to maintain your kids on a health plan, then how can they calculate an appropriate amount of support? If you want to divide up the retirement accounts, but you don't know how many accounts there are or what they are worth, then how can you be expected to properly divide those assets?

Your divorce lawyer needs to be properly prepared for your mediation - if they aren't, this is the single biggest way to waste everyone's time and money.

#2 Have Realistic Expectations About What Divorce Mediation Can Accomplish in Your Case

Prior to attending a mediation with a client, we will prepare a written analysis of every possible issue in your case and give you recommended settlement amounts based on the information we have received up to that point.

This helps our client's to have a realistic expectation about what a financial settlement will look like. If you are looking to receive alimony, we want you to understand what that payment might look like so that you can be prepared when you receive the initial low-ball offer from your spouse. If you think you will see the kids 90% of the time, we want to prepare you for the possibility that you may need to have a joint custody arrangement.

Family law cases are emotionally charged and can be extremely stressful. By setting our client's expectations early on, we can give you time to process so that you are prepared to have some serious and realistic conversations when you walk into the mediator's office.

#3 Mediating Your Case too Soon

A big mistake we frequently see is that couples will attempt to mediate their divorce too soon, before they have a firm understanding about what issues need to be resolved. Many people, in an attempt to save money, will schedule a mediation on their own before they even talk to a lawyer. In other cases, they will make agreements that they can't back out of that are clearly not fair to them.

As I mentioned in #1 above, it is important that you have all the facts and information about your case before you start to talk about settlement options. One you sign and notarize a mediation agreement, there is no going back. Make sure you are fully informed about all aspects of your case before you spend the time and money to attend a mediation. Consulting with a lawyer is a smart investment in this regard.

#4 BUILD IN ROOM TO NEGOTIATE

Another mistake we see people make is that they don't build in room to negotiate with their first settlement offer. This frequently happens with individuals who decide not to hire a divorce lawyer. If their budget says that they can only afford to pay $3,000 in alimony, then the first offer they make is that they will pay $3,000 in alimony, assuming that their spouse will accept that initial offer. But when their spouse counters with a request for $5,000 - they find that they have painted themselves into a corner that they can't get out of.

It is unfortunate, but negotiating the details of a family law case are complicated and there are lots of issues that need to be considered during the process. If you don't have the proper information about what you can and can't accept, then you will spin your wheels trying to reach an agreement, or worse - you will end up with an agreement that is not sustainable long term.

One of the best ways to put yourself in a position to succeed in your divorce mediation is to build in enough room to negotiate what you are willing to accept as your final offer *before* you start to negotiate.

#5 Don't Concede Issues You Don't Care About

With almost every client, there are certain issues they don't care about. It might be the house, or some personal property, or even the amount of alimony. But at the very beginning of the mediation, you don't want to concede those issues because you don't yet undderstand what might be important to your spouse.

Some of the issues that you don't care about may be tremendous issues that your spouse will want to negotiate on. And if that is the case, you will learn that over the course of your negotiation and can "throw in" some of those benefits at the end to reach a final resolution to your case.

You should discuss these issues ahead of time with your lawyer so that you are both on the same page going into the mediation.

How long does a divorce mediation take in North Carolina?

A divorce mediation in North Carolina will frequently take all day, and even last into the evening depending on how complex the case is. In some cases, mediations have been known to last several days or more.

Sometimes the parties will discover, during the course of the mediation, that they need more information about a financial asset or health insurance before they can move forward. In those situations, it is possible to continue the mediation to another day, although this is rare.

HOW MUCH DOES IT COST TO MEDIATE A DIVORCE?

Mediating a family law case is not an inexpensive process, although it is significantly less expensive than hiring a lawyer to prepare a court case and conduct a trial. You will have to pay a lawyer and ½ of the mediator's fee. The rates for the mediator in Wake County run from $175-$350/hour, and there is typically an administrative fee of $200-$250 tacked on. You will be required to pay these fees at the conclusion of the mediation session.

So for an 8-hour mediation, you can expect that your ½ of the mediator's fee will cost anywhere from $800 to $1,500. In addition, you will need to pay your own lawyer for their time attending the mediation, which could run an additional $1,600 to $3,200.

While this seems expensive, you should compare this investment to the investment required to hire a lawyer to prepare for and attend a hearing or trial on your behalf. A good rule of thumb is that it will take a lawyer *at least* 2 hours to prepare for every 1 hour of court time. So if you are paying your lawyer a modest $250 per hour, then a 6 hour hearing (i.e. 1 day in court) would cost approximately $4,500, and this doesn't factor in the cost of expert witnesses, conducting and responding to discovery, and other expenses. By that measure, a mediation is a very good deal.

DO YOU NEED A LAWYER TO GO THROUGH MEDIATION?

No, you do not need a lawyer to go through a mediation in North Carolina, although we highly recommend it. And even if you and your spouse decide to mediate your case without lawyers, you will still want to hire a lawyer to draft your final separation agreement.

A separation agreement is a document that could affect you for years to come - you want to make sure that it is legally sound and accurate. In addition, you want to make sure that the agreement you have reached is in your best interest and that you aren't making a huge mistake that a lawyer would catch had you hired them to review and draft your agreement at the outset.

We frequently meet with clients who have negotiated what they thought were "fair" agreements only to find out that they are receiving way less or paying way more than they should be because they negotiated their agreement without the help of counsel. We also meet with clients who know they are negotiating a bad agreement, but they are so exhausted from the process that they just don't care anymore. In both of these situations, we can help your case get back on track - assuming you haven't already signed and notarized a legally binding agreement.

Mediation is an extremely efficient and cost-effective way to get closure to your case quickly so that you can start the process of moving on with your life. At The Hart Law Firm, we are strong advocates of the mediation process and use it extensively to resolve many of our cases. You would be wise to consider this as an option to resolve your divorce case.

CHAPTER NINE
Collaborative Law

Collaborative Divorce is a new and progressive way for divorcing couples to resolve their disputes peacefully and with respect for one another—without going to court. When couples in North Carolina decide to separate or divorce, they must find a way to resolve all outstanding issues, including Child Custody and Support, Post Separation Support and Alimony, and Property Division (or Equitable Distribution).

Collaborative law is a another method of alternative dispute resolution (ADR) that is designed to minimize the conflict between the parties as they work toward resolving the issues in their case.

In a Collaborative Divorce, each client has the support and counsel of their own attorney. In addition, they may decide to work together, collaboratively, with a team of trained professionals (financial specialists, accountants, therapists, and child counselors) to help them come to win-win, outside the box solutions to any and all disputed aspects of their case.

THE COLLABORATIVE AGREEMENT

A collaborative divorce is distinguished from a traditional divorce in large part by a Participation Agreement that is signed at the beginning of the process by the clients, the attorneys, and any other professionals that are hired to assist with the case. The agreement requires each spouse to complete several steps:

1. **Exchange complete financial information** so that each spouse can make well-informed decisions;

2. **Maintain absolute confidentiality** during the process, so that each spouse can feel free to express his or her needs and concerns;

3. Reach a written agreement on all issues and concerns **without using the court** to decide any contested issues; and,

4. **Mandate the withdrawal** of all professionals (including attorneys) if either client chooses to go to court (except to obtain a final divorce decree).

HOW A COLLABORATIVE DIVORCE WORKS

The first step toward proceeding with a collaborative divorce is that both you and your spouse must agree that this is what you want to do. If either one of you elects to either hire a lawyer who is untrained in the collaborative process, or decides to run to the courthouse to seek judicial relief, then a collaborative divorce is likely to fail.

Once you and your spouse have determined that a collaborative divorce is the appropriate way to proceed, follow the steps below:

First, both spouses must meet with a collaborative attorney to discuss their individual needs and concerns. *A collaborative attorney has received special training in this process. You can't just pick any lawyer off the internet. Make sure to ask if they have completed the collaborative training and ask how many collaborative cases they have handled.*

Second, once each spouse has hired a collaborative attorney, then the couple and their attorneys will meet in a series of four-way sessions to reach a settlement that does not involve the court system. Each meeting is short (roughly two hours) and has a set agenda. Every possible issue—including Property Division, Child Custody and time sharing, Support (both Spousal and Child Support)—is put "on the table" in these sessions. At some of the meetings, other professionals such as Mental Health Professionals and Financial Experts may participate and become part of the "team" to assist the couples jointly in reaching resolutions. Between meetings, the clients may be given "homework" to complete before the following meeting.

Divorcing couples will benefit from the skills, advice, and support of their attorneys and the other professionals while striving to work things out in a positive, resolution-focused manner.

Finally, when a settlement is reached, the attorneys will work together to draft a legal separation agreement that outlines the agreement and intent of the parties.

THE BENEFITS OF COLLABORATIVE DIVORCE

There are multiple benefits to pursuing a collaborative divorce. Some of the most commonly cited benefits include:

Control – You will retain control over your divorce and how it is resolved. Though both you and your spouse each have a lawyer, you will both take responsibility for shaping the settlement as the primary members of the team.

Time – Typically, a collaborative divorce takes less time than a traditional divorce. North Carolina is a perfect state for a collaborative divorce, as a one-year period of separation is required prior to filing for divorce. Many couples can resolve their entire case during the period of separation and finalize the divorce as soon as the one-year separation period is over. With traditional litigation, the issues surrounding the divorce can take many years to resolve, often on terms that are dictated by a judge, not the parties.

Support –You gain support. You craft the settlement cooperatively with your spouse while benefiting from your attorney's advocacy, problem-solving abilities, and negotiating skills. You receive insight and support from other professionals who assist in identifying your interests and your children's needs.

Focus – You can focus on attempting to settle the case, rather than fearing court hearings and legal proceedings. Removing the threat of "going to court" reduces anxiety and fear, thereby helping you focus on finding positive solutions.

Foundation – You lay the foundation for a better future. There is no pain-free way to end a marriage, but by reducing stress, working in a climate of cooperation, and treating each other with respect, both you and your spouse are creating an environment in which you and your children can thrive.

Cost Savings – You get more by combining your resources (i.e., it is not necessary for both you and your spouse to hire each requisite expert—only one is required). As a result, the collaborative process is usually less costly and time-consuming than litigation. When you reach an agreement, it can be finalized within a shorter time frame. You will not get bogged down for months while waiting for a court date.

Customized Settlements – You are able to negotiate a better settlement. Every family is unique and deserves a unique solution to the issues raised in a separation or divorce proceeding. The collaborative process produces final agreements that are frequently more detailed and complete than any order issued by a judge after a contested court proceeding.

Is Collaborative Law Right for Your Case?

Collaborative law empowers a married couple to dissolve their marriage with dignity. Any divorce is ripe for the collaborative process, but you should especially consider collaborative law if both you and your spouse:

- Believe it is important to protect your children from the harm that custody litigation can inflict;

- Place a high value on personal responsibility in resolving conflict;

- Are able to focus on a positive solution for the entire family;

- Want to preserve a respectful working relationship both during and after the process is over; and,

- See the need to disclose full and accurate information about financial issues.

If either of you is unable to work this way, then a collaborative divorce may not be right for you. Furthermore, a number of attorneys will advertise that they are collaborative lawyers, but they have not been fully trained in the collaborative process. If you are just starting to think about your divorce and would like to pursue the collaborative option, it is important for both you and your spouse to find an attorney who is willing to participate in the collaborative process.

At The Hart Law Firm, we have conducted numerous successful collaborative cases over the years. If you have questions about this process and would like to learn more, please feel free to call us at (919) 460-5422 to schedule an initial assessment and go over your personal situation.

SECTION FOUR

UNDERSTANDING THE LEGAL PROCESS

CHAPTER TEN

The Rules of the Game

If you have never been to law school, worked at a law firm, or received any legal training whatsoever, the legal process can seem daunting and confusing. If you attempt to go into court without a lawyer you may feel like the new kid on the block where everyone else already knows everyone, as well as all the inside jokes. You have absolutely no clue what is going on or what everyone is talking about.

In an attempt to help you understand what is going on, here are basic terms you might want to know.

Jurisdiction –This is the legal term that gives the court the legal authority to hear your case. If the court does not have jurisdiction over your case, then it cannot make a decision (a ruling) on your case. There are several types of jurisdiction, and the court must have both to let you proceed with your case. First is subject matter jurisdiction, which means that the court has the legal authority to hear a certain type of case. The second is personal jurisdiction, which means that the court has jurisdiction over you as a party in a lawsuit. Many people make the mistake of thinking that all courts and cases are the same—and that is simply not the case.

In North Carolina, the District Court has jurisdiction to hear family law cases, including claims for Child Custody and support, Equitable Distribution, Alimony, Post Separation Support, Divorce from Bed and Board, and Absolute Divorce.

Complaint – In order for a court to hear your case, you must open up a court file. You do this by filing a "complaint" with the clerk of court in your county. A complaint tells the court who the parties are in your case (typically you and your spouse), why the court has jurisdiction over your case, and what relief you are seeking from the court, such as Alimony or Child Custody.

Service of Process – When you file your complaint, the clerk will issue a "summons." A summons is a legal document that informs your spouse that you have filed a complaint against them. You are responsible for making sure that your spouse is "served" with the complaint, summons, and any other documents you filed at the time you filed the complaint (such as a notice of hearing, custody order, etc.). In most cases, this can be done by mailing a copy of the lawsuit and summons to your spouse via certified mail, with return receipt requested. You may also pay the sheriff to serve the lawsuit, or you can hire a private process server.

Answer – After the complaint is served on the defendant, the defendant has thirty days in North Carolina to respond to that complaint. The response can take the form of a motion or, more commonly, an answer. The answer will admit or deny the allegations in the complaint. If the complaint is legally insufficient, the defendant can file a motion to dismiss the complaint in lieu of an answer.

Financial Disclosures – In Family Court, where there are financial issues to be decided, each county in North Carolina has a different set of rules about what documents must automatically be disclosed to the other party. These documents typically include income information, tax returns, bank statements, credit card statements, retirement accounts, and other related documents.

Discovery – In some cases, the financial disclosures are insufficient to provide a clear picture of the financial circumstances of the parties. When this happens, a lawyer may send discovery to the other party. Discovery most frequently takes the form of written questions or "interrogatories" and requests for production of documents. However, discovery can also include a request for admissions or even a deposition, which is where a party is asked to answer questions under oath in the presence of a court reporter.

Subpoenas – a subpoena is a legal document that requires a person or entity to either appear and provide testimony or provide written documents. If you hire a lawyer to help with your case, they are permitted to sign subpoenas on their own. However, if you represent yourself, you must ask the clerk or a judge to sign a subpoena on your behalf.

Motions – Motions are filed to ask the court to issue an order on a court file. As discussed previously, you can file a motion to dismiss which asks the court to dismiss a lawsuit. You can also file a motion asking the court to compel the other party to do something such as produce financial disclosures when they have failed to follow the local rules in your county. If someone files a motion in your case, a hearing will need to be scheduled for the court to rule on that motion.

Consent Order – A consent order is a court order that is "consented to" by all parties in a case. For example, if you and your spouse reach a settlement in a contested case, your lawyer can draft a consent order that everyone will sign. Once signed by all the parties, it will be sent to the judge to sign without the need for a hearing or a trial.

Hearing – When a party to a case files a motion, a hearing is required. A hearing can take two forms, evidentiary and non-evidentiary. An evidentiary hearing will require testimony from witnesses and possibly the introduction of documentary evidence. Temporary hearings on custody and support issues are usually evidentiary hearings. A non-evidentiary hearing is the presentation of legal arguments from both parties. In both cases, the judge will issue a ruling, that is, they will make a decision to grant or deny the motion.

Trial – A trial is very similar to a hearing but is much longer and will make a final disposition of the issues raised in the complaint. A trial is always an evidentiary proceeding and will require the testimony of the parties, expert witnesses, other witnesses, and the introduction of documentary evidence.

WHO SHOULD FILE FIRST?

The question of who should file legal paperwork first depends in large part on your unique personal situation and what is meant by "filing" legal paperwork. In North Carolina, when we refer to "filing for divorce," you could be referring to filing for the Absolute Divorce or filing for any of the other legal remedies you may be seeking (i.e., Post Separation Support, Alimony, Equitable Distribution, Attorney's Fees, Child Custody, Child Support, etc.).

If we are discussing the sole act of filing for Absolute Divorce after the other issues have been resolved, then it does not matter who files the paperwork. In most of these types of cases, the Absolute Divorce is filed as a "friendly" lawsuit, meaning that it is only filed because you need the court to grant the divorce both parties desire, with no contested issues.

On the other hand, if you have just recently separated or are thinking about separating, then the question of who should file legal paperwork first is more important. From a purely legal standpoint, it does not much matter who files first. Both you and your spouse will have an opportunity to have your case heard, and there is no significant tactical advantage at trial to be the one that filed first.

Practically, however, the party that files first is referred to as the "plaintiff" in North Carolina (in other states they may be referred to as the "petitioner" or even "Husband/Wife"), and the person receiving the documents is referred to as the "defendant" (in other states, they may be referred to as the "respondent"). This may be important to you.

Another significant difference is that the person filing the legal paperwork has the opportunity to present their evidence first at the trial or hearing. Although very few cases proceed to a hearing or trial, if yours does, this could be a slight advantage, as your attorney will tell your side of the story to the judge first. You may want to file first for additional reasons:

- You have more time to prepare your financial disclosures;

- You may be able to have some say when the court date is for temporary matters;

- You may catch your spouse off-guard, not expecting the lawsuit and ill-prepared to represent themselves at a temporary hearing;

- Your spouse may be served by the sheriff, which can be an unnerving process; and,

- You do not need to worry about when or if your spouse is going to file, and then scramble to respond to their complaint (you only have thirty days to respond to a lawsuit, which is a surprisingly short amount of time).

When I am counseling clients about whether to file a lawsuit or not, I look at a number of factors, including these:

- Is the client in need of immediate financial support?

- Is there a substantial risk that the other party will hide or dispose of assets?

- Is there a risk that another party will flee with the children?

- Are the parties working together to try to reach an amicable settlement?

- Are the parties willing to voluntarily exchange financial documents without a court order?

- Are the parties able to work out a custody schedule on their own?

Generally speaking, if I have a client in need of immediate financial support, and their spouse is not voluntarily providing support, then it is more important to file a lawsuit sooner rather than later. In some counties in North Carolina, it can take six to nine months or longer to schedule a hearing with a judge to decide temporary support.

Most spouses that require support do not have the time to wait and see if their spouse will voluntarily pay an appropriate amount of Post Separation Support or Alimony. And even if they do, without a court order or signed separation agreement, there is nothing to prevent the paying spouse from unilaterally terminating those monthly payments whenever they wish.

However, in cases where both spouses are working together toward an agreement, voluntarily exchanging financial documents and working out a custody schedule on their own, there is less need to involve the court system.

CHAPTER ELEVEN
How to Get Divorced in North Carolina

Many people get confused when discussing how to get divorced in North Carolina. This is because in North Carolina, as opposed to other states, filing for divorce can only happen after you have been legally separated for a year, and is a completely separate process than dividing up property or determining an appropriate level of spousal support.

When you get a final divorce in North Carolina, it is called an Absolute Divorce.[3] In this chapter we will review the legal requirements to obtain an Absolute Divorce in North Carolina, and discuss how to start this process.

LEGAL REQUIREMENTS FOR AN ABSOLUTE DIVORCE

It is relatively easy to obtain a divorce in North Carolina, so long as you can wait out the one year separation requirement. As discussed in other chapters, in North Carolina you must be *physically separated* from your spouse for one full year before you can file for divorce. In addition, either you or your spouse must have been a resident of North Carolina for six months prior to

---

[3] The Absolute Divorce should not be confused with a Divorce from Bed and Board, which is discussed in a later chapter.

the date that one of you files for divorce.[4] Let's take these two issues one at a time.

First, you must show the court that you have been physically separated for one full year. That means that you cannot live in separate bedrooms in the same house. One of you cannot have moved out for six months, then came back for a month, and then left for another six months—that starts the clock ticking again.

A frequent question I am asked is whether having sex with your spouse during the separation period will cause the statutory clock to start over. Under North Carolina Statutes,[5] the answer is no, but you must be careful not to "resume marital relations." In other words, one crazy drunken night during the separation period would not restart the clock, but if it becomes habitual, then it may indeed rise to a resumption of marital relations.

Second, either you or your spouse must have been a resident of North Carolina for six months prior to filing the complaint for Absolute Divorce. What is important to note here is that one of you could leave the state and still file for and get divorced in North Carolina. If both of you move out of North Carolina prior to filing for divorce, however, then you cannot obtain the divorce in North Carolina.

Assuming that you can meet those two requirements, obtaining a divorce is a relatively easy matter but not without significant consequences. Simply put, an Absolute Divorce in North Carolina is simply a change in legal status—one day you

---

[4] N.C.G.S. § 50-6
[5] N.C.G.S. § 52-10.2

are married, and the next day you are not. You do not need to worry about division of property, Child Custody arrangements, or spousal support (i.e., Alimony) in the divorce proceeding.

That is not to say that there are not implications to ending your marriage. You will give up important statutory rights and may lose access to health insurance if covered by your spouse's plan. You will also give up your right to request spousal support from your spouse or to have the court divide your marital property if you do not have these claims pending when the judgment of Absolute Divorce is entered.

For these reasons, I highly recommend that you discuss these issues with a family law attorney before you file for an Absolute Divorce or immediately upon receiving a complaint for Absolute Divorce from your spouse or their attorney.

Provided that the filing is done properly, there are no issues with service of process, and the Absolute Divorce is uncontested, most Absolute Divorces are granted within sixty to ninety days of filing. A frequent source of confusion in North Carolina is the distinction between an Absolute Divorce and a Divorce from Bed and Board. A Divorce from Bed and Board is a fault-based process by which an injured spouse can ask the court to order the other spouse out of the marital residence, thereby starting the one-year separation period. I will address this topic in a later section.

STARTING THE PROCESS

Starting the divorce process in North Carolina is not always as clear cut as one might think. In some cases, the decision to divorce is mutual and reached by both spouses together after years of fighting and counseling. In other cases, one spouse falls out of love with the other and tells them they are through with the marriage—sometimes in a fit of anger after a long, exhausting fight. In still other cases, one spouse simply moves out and leaves a note while the other spouse is out, leaving the one left behind confused and bewildered.

I have seen all these scenarios and many others. Even though each situation is unique, at the end of the day they all share one common characteristic: the process of divorce has begun, and each spouse is starting to think about their individual futures. What will happen with the kids? Will they be okay financially? Can they afford to part with half of their retirement savings? What will happen to their small business?

Because many attorneys counsel their clients to stay put in the marital home until a separation agreement is signed, oftentimes there is not much that can be done in the court system in the early days of the divorce process. In order to file a claim for Post Separation Support, Alimony, or Equitable Distribution, the parties must be physically separated. As discussed previously, even though claims for Post Separation Support and Alimony can be "piggy-backed" to a claim for Divorce from Bed and Board (i.e., DBB), in DBB cases you must show some sort of fault. If no one is at fault, there is no legal way to force the other spouse out of the marital home and thereby begin the process of filing a divorce-related lawsuit.

So, what do you do in these situations? Many people start by meeting with a divorce attorney to begin mapping out a legal strategy. The first stage of this process is to take stock of your finances and begin gathering your financial documents. If the divorce is mutual, you can start to talk to your spouse about what the settlement will look like. If, however, you are seeking a divorce and have not yet told your spouse, you will probably want to discuss your legal rights with a family law attorney before you discuss the possibility of divorce with your spouse. You will want to carefully review the twelve steps to prepare for divorce later in this book.

At these early days of the process, it is possible that a settlement can be reached out of court either with or without the assistance of a lawyer. The more complicated your marital estate and support needs, the more likely it is that you will need a lawyer to help you through this process. If you are able to reach an amicable settlement, then you and your spouse can sign what is commonly referred to as a "separation agreement and Property Settlement." After you and your spouse have signed this agreement in front of a notary, one of you will be required to move out of the marital home within thirty (30) days for the agreement to become binding.

WORD OF WARNING: DO NOT SIGN ANY LEGAL DOCUMENTS PROVIDED BY YOUR SPOUSE OR HIS/HER ATTORNEY UNTIL YOU HAVE HAD ANOTHER ATTORNEY REVIEW THEM FOR YOU FIRST. YOU COULD BE GIVING UP VALUABLE LEGAL RIGHTS IF YOU DO SO.

If you are unable to reach an agreement with your spouse, someone will have to move out of the house to initiate a legal action. A legal action is started when the plaintiff files what is called a complaint with the clerk of court in your county and paying the requisite fees (typically $150 to $225). A complaint is simply a document outlining the basis for the court to take jurisdiction in your case and outlines for the court the legal basis for the remedies you seek.

When you file the complaint, you must also prepare three original copies of a "civil summons" for the clerk to execute. In addition, the local rules in your county may require you to file other documents, such as a civil cover sheet, a notice of hearing for temporary matters, a judicial assignment form, an order to attend mediation in custody cases, and other assorted documents. You will need to check your local rules, which can be found at www.nccourts.org by searching under your specific county.

Once a lawsuit is filed, your spouse must be "served" with a copy of the documents that were filed, as well as a copy of the summons signed by the clerk. You have sixty days from the date that the summons was issued to properly serve your spouse in accordance with the North Carolina Rules of Civil Procedure. Typically, this is done by providing a copy of the lawsuit and original summons to the sheriff's office in your county and paying a nominal fee to have a sheriff personally serve the documents for you.

Once your spouse has been served, he or she has thirty days to file a response. When they file a response, they will typically include "counter-claims," which are essentially their version of the complaint that you filed, but with added requests from the court to award them specific relief. There are many other important deadlines for the disclosure of financial documents tied to the date you filed your lawsuit or the date your spouse was served. If you decide to hire a divorce lawyer to help you, they will know these deadlines backward and forward. If you decide to represent yourself, you must check with your local county rules to determine what those deadlines are.

One other word of warning. Complaints can be vicious, mean documents. You may have a hard time with the allegations contained in them. Just because someone says something in a complaint does not mean it is true, nor does it mean that the facts claimed can even be proven by your spouse in court. Many attorneys give intimate details of the case in their complaints—but do not let this bother you. I see this as an advantage for my clients because it gives some insight into what the other attorney is going to try to prove at trial.

CHAPTER TWELVE

Spousal Support and Alimony

Alimony in North Carolina is a payment from one spouse (the "supporting spouse") to another spouse (the "dependent spouse"). In general, the supporting spouse is the spouse that earns more income than the dependent spouse. There are sixteen factors in the North Carolina statutes that will guide the judge on making a decision about whether or not to award Alimony, how much Alimony to award, and for how long. I have listed these factors below:[6]

1. The marital misconduct of either of the spouses. Nothing herein shall prevent a court from considering incidents of post date-of-separation marital misconduct as corroborating evidence supporting other evidence that marital misconduct occurred during the marriage and prior to date of separation;

2. The relative earnings and earning capacities of the spouses;

3. The ages and the physical, mental, and emotional conditions of the spouses;

---

[6] N.C.G.S. § 50-16.3A(b)

4. The amount and sources of earned and unearned income of both spouses, including, but not limited to, earnings, dividends, and benefits such as medical, retirement, insurance, social security, or others;

5. The duration of the marriage;

6. The contribution by one spouse to the education, training, or increased earning power of the other spouse;

7. The extent to which the earning power, expenses, or financial obligations of a spouse will be affected by reason of serving as the custodian of a minor child;

8. The standard of living of the spouses established during the marriage;

9. The relative education of the spouses and the time necessary to acquire sufficient education or training to enable the spouse seeking Alimony to find employment to meet his or her reasonable economic needs;

10. The relative assets and liabilities of the spouses and the relative debt service requirements of the spouses, including legal obligations of support;

11. The property brought to the marriage by either spouse;

12. The contribution of a spouse as homemaker;

13. The relative needs of the spouses;

14. The federal, state, and local tax ramifications of the Alimony award;

15. Any other factor relating to the economic circumstances of the parties that the court finds to be just and proper;

16. The fact that income received by either party was previously considered by the court in determining the value of a marital or divisible asset in an Equitable Distribution of the parties' marital or divisible property.

Alimony falls under the general category of "spousal support" in North Carolina. Because residents of North Carolina must wait at least one year before obtaining a divorce, spousal support can take on two separate forms: pre-divorce and post-divorce. Spousal support paid prior to the date of Absolute Divorce is typically referred to as Post Separation Support, or PSS. Spousal support paid after the date of divorce is typically referred to as Alimony.

The amount of Alimony to be paid can vary widely depending on the circumstances of the case. Typically, the court will look at the budgetary "need" of the dependent spouse and compare that to the "ability to pay" of the supporting spouse. When determining the financial needs of a dependent spouse, the court will look at the parties' accustomed standard of living in the last several years before separation.

A dependent spouse seeking Alimony is not required to deplete his or her individual assets in order to maintain the parties' accustomed standard of living. The ability to pay is calculated by looking at the reasonable budgeted expenses of the supporting spouse and subtracting those from the income of the supporting spouse. The surplus, if any, can be used to offset the financial need of the dependent spouse. While this is a broad overgeneralization, it is still a good starting point to determine the amount of Alimony required.

WHEN CAN I SUE?

An action for Post Separation Support or Alimony may be brought in conjunction with a claim for Absolute Divorce, Divorce from Bed and Board, or as an independent action whether or not a separate action for divorce is pending. Typically, the parties must be separated in order to file an independent claim for Post Separation Support.

However, the parties must still be married on the date that a claim for Post Separation Support or Alimony is filed. If you get divorced without previously filing a claim for PSS or Alimony, or you did file a claim *but the claim is no longer pending on the date of divorce*, then you will lose the legal right to seek a resolution of your Alimony or Post Separation Support claim in court.

DO I HAVE TO GO TO COURT?

No. Alimony and Post Separation Support can both be, and typically are, settled out of court in the form of a negotiated separation agreement or consent order.

HOW LONG DO SUPPORT PAYMENTS LAST?

This depends on whether the support payment is considered Alimony or Post Separation Support. Post-separation support will typically terminate upon the date of divorce or entry of an order on Alimony. Alimony, on the other hand, will terminate on a date provided for by the court (usually, but not always, half the term of the marriage through the date of separation). In addition, Alimony will terminate, pursuant to the applicable statutes[7], if:

1. The parties resume marital relations;

2. The dependent spouse remarries;

3. The dependent spouse cohabits with another adult in a private heterosexual or homosexual relationship;

4. The dependent spouse dies; or,

5. The supporting spouse dies.

If the issue of spousal support is decided by execution of a negotiated separation and property settlement agreement, the parties may negotiate the payment for whatever termination conditions they wish.

ALIMONY AND TAXES...

Beginning in 2019, alimony is no longer taxable to the receiving spouse, nor is it tax deductible to the paying spouse. So no, you do not need to pay taxes on the alimony you receive and if you are paying alimony, you do not get to deduct it on your tax return. This will certainly impact how you negotiate your spousal support payments.

HOW WILL MARITAL MISCONDUCT AFFECT SUPPORT?

In North Carolina, the party requesting Alimony does not need to prove marital fault or misconduct on the part of the supporting spouse in order to receive Alimony. However, fault is

---

[7] N.C.G.S. § 50-16.9(b)

a factor that can play a role in the determination of whether a spouse will have to pay Alimony.

If the dependent spouse engaged in acts of un-condoned illicit sexual behavior with a third party, then they are legally barred from receiving Alimony (but not Post Separation Support) unless their spouse has condoned (or forgiven them) for their conduct.

Conversely, if it is a close call as to whether or not the supporting spouse should have to pay Alimony, but they had an affair without being forgiven, then the court must order them to pay Alimony.

One final scenario that you should be aware of: if both spouses engaged in marital misconduct during the marriage (and prior to separation), then the courts will evaluate the case as if there was no marital misconduct and will look to the sixteen factors enumerated above.

Either party may request a jury trial on the issue of marital misconduct.

CHAPTER THIRTEEN
Dividing Up Your Assets

In North Carolina, the process of dividing your property is known as Equitable Distribution. There are two requirements for filing an Equitable Distribution claim: 1) you must be married to the person you are filing the claim against; and, 2) you must be separated from them on the date you file the claim for Equitable Distribution. If either of these two requirements are not met, the court will lack jurisdiction to hear your claim and a motion to dismiss would be proper.

It is important to note that you must file your claim for Equitable Distribution *before* your divorce is granted. If you fail to do so, then you will lose the right to go to court for a division of your property.

It is common for divorcing couples to resolve all issues related to Equitable Distribution in a separation agreement.

EQUITABLE DISTRIBUTION STATUTORY FACTORS
According to N.C.G.S. § 50-20(c), there shall be an equal division by using net value of marital property and net value of divisible property unless the court determines that an equal division is not equitable. If the court determines that an equal division is

not equitable, the court shall divide the marital property and divisible property equitably. The court shall consider the following factors under this subsection:

1. The income, property, and liabilities of each party at the time the division of property is to become effective.

2. Any obligation for support arising out of a prior marriage.

3. The duration of the marriage and the age and physical and mental health of both parties.

4. The need of a parent with custody of a child or children of the marriage to occupy or own the marital residence and to use or own its household effects.

5. The expectation of pension, retirement, or other deferred compensation rights that are not marital property.

6. Any equitable claim to, interest in, or direct or indirect contribution made to the acquisition of such marital property by the party not having title, including joint efforts or expenditures and contributions and services, or lack thereof, as a spouse, parent, wage earner, or homemaker.

7. Any direct or indirect contribution made by one spouse to help educate or develop the career potential of the other spouse.

8. Any direct contribution to an increase in value of separate property which occurs during the course of the marriage.

9. The liquid or nonliquid character of all marital property and divisible property.

10. The difficulty of evaluating any component asset or any interest in a business, corporation, or profession, and the economic desirability of retaining such asset or interest intact and free from any claim or interference by the other party.

11. The tax consequences to each party, including those federal and state tax consequences that would have been incurred if the marital and divisible property had been sold or liquidated on the date of valuation. The trial court may, however, in its discretion, consider whether or when such tax consequences are reasonably likely to occur in determining the equitable value deemed appropriate for this factor.

a. Acts of either party to maintain, preserve, develop, or expand; or to waste, neglect, devalue, or convert the marital property or divisible property, or both, during the period after separation of the parties and before the time of distribution.

b. In the event of the death of either party prior to the entry of any order for the distribution of property made pursuant to this subsection:

i. Property passing to the surviving spouse by will or through intestacy due to the death of a spouse.

ii. Property held as tenants by the entirety or as joint tenants with rights of survivorship passing to the surviving spouse due to the death of a spouse.

iii. Property passing to the surviving spouse from life insurance, individual retirement accounts, pension or profit-sharing plans, any private or governmental retirement plan or annuity of which the decedent controlled the designation of beneficiary (excluding any benefits under the federal social security system), or any other retirement accounts or contracts, due to the death of a spouse.

iv. The surviving spouse's right to claim an "elective share" pursuant to G.S. 30-3.1 through G.S. 30-33, unless otherwise waived.

12.   Any other factor which the court finds to be just and proper.

The Role of Marital Fault

North Carolina does not consider marital fault or misconduct when dividing marital assets unless it has an economic impact on the financial condition of the spouses. In other words, the fact that your spouse had an affair is not going to affect how your property is divided, but if your spouse spent significant marital assets on the affair, then it may have an effect.

Equitable Distribution Analysis

In deciding how to divide up your marital estate, the courts follow a straightforward analysis. First, the courts must classify all your property. The court can choose from three classifications of property:

Marital Property. This is property that was acquired by either spouse during the marriage and before the date of separation of the parties and that is presently owned. There are nuances and complexities in this definition that are, frankly, outside the scope of this book.

Separate Property. Property acquired before the marriage, property acquired by gift or inheritance during the marriage, and professional and business licenses that would terminate on transfer.

Divisible Property. This is property received by the parties after the date of separation up to the date of distribution. Typically, divisible property amounts to passive increases or decreases in the value of marital property or debts, or passive income that is derived from marital property.

Once the court has classified the property, the next step is to place a value on the marital and divisible property. Marital property will be valued as of the date of separation, while divisible property will be valued as of the date that the court distributes the property.

Finally, the court must distribute the property "equitably." Equitably typically means equally, but there are exceptions where an equal division will not necessarily be equitable. The court considers the twelve factors listed previously when dividing up the marital and divisible property, including income of the parties, length of the marriage, liquid or non-liquid character of property, and basically any other factor the court would like to consider.

SOURCE OF FUNDS RULE

North Carolina follows what is known as the "source of funds" rule when classifying if a particular asset is or is not marital property. What this means is that the court will look at the *source of funds* used to acquire a certain property to determine if it is marital or separate property.

For example, if you purchase a new car *after* you are separated from your spouse, then according to the definition of marital property, this car would not qualify. However, if the car was purchased with cash that was drawn out of a marital bank account, since the source of the funds used to purchase the car was marital, then the car itself is marital property also. The implication of this rule is that you can have property that is both marital and separate in nature.

HOW TO DIVIDE A FAMILY BUSINESS

Aside from the marital home and retirement accounts, the family business can be one of the largest investments that must be divided in a divorce case. If you and your spouse are both working for the business, things can be especially tricky. If you have a family business and are considering divorce, it is better for you to seek the help of an attorney sooner rather than later so that you can engage in some pre-divorce planning.

The first step in dividing the family business is to start to think about how it is going to be divided. Will you and your spouse continue to co-own the business, will it be sold, or will one of you buy out the other?

The next important (and often overlooked) step is to determine the value of the business. Just as we typically hire an appraiser to put a value on the marital home, you may need to hire a certified appraiser to value the business. This is especially important as the value of the business, depending on whether you or your spouse is going to receive the business, can vary dramatically.

Finally, a hoard of additional issues must be considered when a family business is concerned, including:

- When was the business created, and by whom?

- How many other family members may be involved in running the business?

- What percentage of the business is owned by you and/or your spouse?

- What is the corporate structure of the business?

- Is this even a business at all—in other words, could the business owner step away from the business and still earn a living?

- What outstanding liabilities (including taxes) is the business responsible for?

- Is a confidentiality agreement or buy-sell agreement going to be necessary?

- Did you sign a pre- or post-nuptial agreement with your spouse that covers the division of the business in the event of divorce?

- Is there a business partnership agreement or shareholder agreement that would address what happens in the event of divorce?

- Is there a way to structure a buyout of the business in periodic payments so as to minimize disruption to the business?

- If you are the business owner, you may want to consider timing your divorce and separation at a point where the business has a lower valuation.

- Are you or your spouse liable for any personal guarantees?

- What are the tax consequences of transferring the business?

CHAPTER FOURTEEN
Child Custody and Support

If you are a parent, one of your biggest concerns is who will have custody of your children.

Whenever we talk about custody in North Carolina, it is important to distinguish between legal custody and physical custody. Legal custody refers to who gets the right to make everyday decisions for your children. These choices may include what school your children attend, if they will go to church, and what extracurricular activities they may participate in. In addition, you may need to make decisions regarding the health and well-being of your child. These decisions are decided by the parent who has legal custody of the child. Unless there are extenuating circumstances (such as if one parent is incarcerated or domestic violence was involved in the relationship), typically both parents are awarded joint legal custody.

The other type of custody is physical custody. When you decide to separate and divorce, you and your spouse must decide how physical custody will be shared. Physical custody can be (a) joint—both parents have approximately equal time with the children, (b) split—each parent is the primary parent for a different child, or, most commonly, (c) one parent is the primary physical parent and the other parent has visitation with the minor children.

You can be as creative as you want when it comes to physical custody. A myriad of custodial schedules can be used. When negotiating custody, the most important consideration is what will be in the best interest of the minor children. Secondarily, you must consider what will work for you and the other parent.

Custody can be negotiated as part of your separation agreement, or it will be decided by a district court judge. We strongly urge our clients to come to an agreement out of court regarding what is best for their children. A contentious custody case can be extremely harmful for your minor children. The more you can work together with the other parent to negotiate a schedule that works for everyone, the better the situation will be for your children.

Divorce is disruptive enough for a family, especially in North Carolina where one spouse is forced to move out of the marital residence. This causes the children to split time between two households, and without a parenting plan in place, it can be extremely stressful and unpredictable.

When negotiating a parenting plan, you will want to clearly state who will be the primary physical parent and how often visitation will occur with the other parent. You may want to negotiate who will be responsible for pick-ups and drop-offs, and what will happen if one parent cannot care for the children during their designated custodial time.

You may also want to include language in your agreement that makes it clear that neither parent is to disparage the other in the presence of the children, as well as discuss how soon you will introduce the children to future boyfriends or girlfriends. The bottom line is that the more detailed you can make your agreement, the easier it will be everyone involved.

Child custody is often settled by execution of a voluntary separation agreement between the parties. Other cases can be resolved through the use of court-ordered mediation. Child custody is highly emotional and can quickly become extremely expensive. Focus on what is in the best interests of the child. The court will work off of this standard. With the exception of vary rare cases, your child will not have a say in the process. Judges are loath to bring a child into the courtroom, as are most good attorneys. If you find an attorney that wants to bring in your ten-year-old to testify, run the other way.

JURISDICTION

North Carolina, like many other states, has adopted the Uniform Child Custody Jurisdiction and Enforcement Act (UCCJEA) that governs jurisdiction for Child Custody matters. The purpose of the UCCJEA is to provide stability in Child Custody proceedings and prevent forum shopping by a parent that is disgruntled with the court process.

The UCCJEA gives a child's home state continuing and exclusive jurisdiction over custody matters. There is an elaborate and complicated statutory scheme used to determine which state will be the home state of the minor child, which is beyond the scope of this book. Suffice it to say, if the child has resided in North Carolina for at least six months prior to instituting a Child

Custody action, then North Carolina will have home state jurisdiction to make decisions regarding Child Custody.

INITIATING A CHILD CUSTODY ACTION

To initiate a Child Custody action, one parent must file a complaint in the district court in the county where one of the parties resides. This is typically the county where the child also resides, but it need not be.

A Child Custody action is unique under Chapter 50 of the North Carolina Statutes in that the parties need not be separated for a custody action to be commenced. The reason for this is to promote stability and predictability for the children that are subject to the proceeding. If one parent moves out without a Child Custody order in place, it can lead to chaos and confusion regarding the schedule for the child, issues with where they will go to school, and other problems. We commonly recommend that parents file a custody action in certain situations:

They are being denied visitation by the other parent;

They fear that the other parent will flee the jurisdiction with the child; or,

There is continued fighting over which parent should be the primary physical parent and they cannot reach consensus regarding visitation.

One of benefits of filing a custody lawsuit is that many counties in North Carolina will allow access to court-mandated custody mediation. This gives you an opportunity to try to work out your custodial issues with a neutral third party before your case is heard before a judge.

BEST INTEREST RULE

If you are unable to resolve your case in custody mediation, your case will be assigned to a judge and scheduled for a temporary hearing. These hearings are governed by the local rules in your county and typically last anywhere from one to two hours.

During this hearing, both parents will have an opportunity to present their case to a district court judge and convince them that it would be in the "best interests" of the minor child that the judge award them custody. Evidence will be taken, typically in the form of oral testimony, from both parents.

I realize it is hard to fully understand what goes on in the courtroom unless you have been there before, but one hour to present your entire case is not that much time. You will need to divide this time between opening and closing statements, your testimony, the testimony of any other witnesses you would like to question, and your cross-examination of your spouse and their witnesses. Attorneys are trained to make the most of this time so that you present only the most important evidence and don't run out of time in the middle of your case.

After both parties have presented their evidence, the judge judge will make a ruling on the issue of temporary custody. You are not permitted to appeal temporary custody orders in North Carolina. If neither parent schedules a permanent custody hearing within a year, the temporary ruling will become a permanent custody order.

CHILD CUSTODY MODIFICATION – AN OVERVIEW

If you have an existing Child Custody order that is not working for you or your children, then you may need to change it. Unfortunately, you cannot just unilaterally decide that you do not like the order anymore, even if you consented to the order originally (as most parents do). The good news is that, in certain circumstances, you can request a Child Custody modification in North Carolina. Here is what you need to know to do this.

This section assumes that you are attempting to modify a North Carolina Child Custody Order and the child that is subject to the order still resides in North Carolina. If your child has lived elsewhere for more than six months, then you have what lawyers like to call a "jurisdictional" dilemma.

A complex set of rules and procedures govern where the motion for Child Custody modification can be filed, depending on where the child currently lives. These rules are outside the scope of this book. However, if the child still lives in North Carolina where the original order was entered, then your case will be more straight-forward.

Second, you must have an actual order that would need to be modified. A Child Custody order means that a court file was opened and an order was entered (i.e., signed) by a judge. Many people will file a Child Custody action, but then resolve the case outside of court (typically via a separation agreement) and dismiss the Child Custody action. In this situation, you would not be seeking a Child Custody modification, but rather would be requesting an initial Child Custody determination.

I realize this seems confusing, but the takeaway is that to request a Child Custody modification, you must have a valid

Child Custody order already in place. If you are not sure if you have one, I recommend going to your local clerk of court, pulling your old Child Custody file (or files), and checking to see if there is a valid Child Custody order in the court file.

LEGAL REQUIREMENT TO MODIFY CUSTODY

Just because the child lives in North Carolina and you have a valid Child Custody order in place does not mean you are legally permitted to modify that order. You must meet certain legal requirements to request a Child Custody modification. Typically, there is a two-step test:

1. Has there been a substantial change in circumstances since the original Child Custody order was entered?

2. Would modifying the Child Custody order be in the child's best interest?

A few examples can illustrate a "substantial change in circumstances" that would warrant a change of custody:

- The existing order was entered when the child was preschool age, but now the child is older and the former schedule no longer works;

- One parent has lost a job and/or been forced to move away;

- One parent continually and habitually fails to follow the existing order;

- One parent has developed significant health problems that impact their ability to parent or take care of the child; or,

- One parent has gone to jail and/or prison.

There may be more than one factor in play that would tend to show the court that a substantial change in circumstances has occurred. The motion for modification needs to set out clearly what substantial change in circumstances has occurred.

Next, you must allege in the motion that the modification would be in the child's best interest. This is the most important factor for any judge hearing a Child Custody case—and is something that you must understand. When you go into court requesting anything related to custody, there is no guarantee about what the court might do. If the court finds that there has been a substantial change in circumstances, the judge could agree that your proposed schedule is in the children's best interest, or the judge could agree with the proposal of the other parent. Or, the judge could come up with a schedule of their own that they think would be in the child's best interest.

In addition, you are permitted to request Attorney's Fees in conjunction with a motion to modify Child Custody. If you think you need help paying for your lawyer, and your child's other parent is in a position to afford to pay your legal fees, you will want to include this request in your motion. If you hire a lawyer to assist you, they will typically include the request for Attorney's Fees in the motion they draft.

CHILD SUPPORT

As with custody, Child Support can be agreed to by both parents in a separation agreement. Child support should be relatively easy to negotiate as North Carolina has a statutory scheme for determining the amount of Child Support that should be paid based on the number of children, the visitation schedule, and the income of the parties.

Other factors that can play a role in the Child Support calculation include the cost of health insurance and work-related childcare for the minor children, whether either parent has another child that they must support, and any other extraordinary expenses for the children.

DURATION OF CHILD SUPPORT

Child support will typically stay in effect until a child turns eighteen years of age, unless they are still in high school, in which case Child Support will continue until the child graduates or turns twenty, whichever comes first. Alternatively, if the child is emancipated before they turn age 18, then Child Support will terminate at that time.

If you owe a duty of Child Support for more than one child, when the older child turns eighteen, you will need to seek a Child Support modification to terminate that portion of your Child Support order. Child support does not terminate automatically in North Carolina as it does in other states.

CHAPTER FIFTEEN

Divorce from Bed and Board

In North Carolina, a Divorce from Bed and Board is available to ask the courts to force a legal separation. Do not confuse it with the Absolute Divorce—if a judge grants a Divorce from Bed and Board, you are not legally divorced. Rather, you become legally separated from your spouse, and one of you will be ordered to vacate the marital home.

In order to obtain a Divorce from Bed and Board, you must show that your spouse is "at fault". This means that you must allege one of the following grounds for the court to grant the Divorce from Bed and Board:

- Abandonment

- Malicious turning out of doors

- Cruel or barbarous treatment endangering the life of the other

- Indignities that render the complaining spouse's condition intolerable or live overly burdensome

- Excessive drug or alcohol use

- Adultery

Whether or not your spouse has engaged in activities that give you sufficient grounds for a Divorce from Bed and Board is highly fact-dependent to your specific situation. I recommend that my clients keep a journal of specific dates and actions when their spouse did things that make their life burdensome or intolerable so that they can start building a case against their spouse if it becomes necessary to file a Divorce from Bed and Board.

At the time you file the Divorce from Bed and Board, you can ask the court to decide a number of other issues, including Post Separation Support, Alimony, Child Custody, and Child Support. (Please note that you cannot file a claim for Equitable Distribution until after you and your spouse have physically separated).

A quick word of warning: it can often take a long time to get a hearing in front of a judge on your claim for Divorce from Bed and Board. Each North Carolina county is different, and you should consult with a family law attorney in your county to determine just how long it might take to schedule a hearing with a judge where you live. The longer it might take to get a hearing, the earlier you will want to start settlement negotiations and, possibly, legal proceedings.

SECTION FIVE

HIRING THE RIGHT LAWYER

CHAPTER SIXTEEN

Do You Even Need a Lawyer?

You have made the decision to separate from your spouse. In North Carolina, this is a preliminary step that must take place before you can obtain a divorce. You may or may not have discussed this decision with your spouse. Either way, you do not know what to do next. How do you decide? Well, you need to look at a variety of factors, such as:

Assets/Liabilities – Do you and/or your spouse have a lot of assets (i.e. stocks, bonds, investment properties, 401(k), etc.) to split up? Conversely, do you have debts that you need to divide?

Children – Is custody going to be an issue? Do you need to calculate Child Support?

Home – Do you own your home or rent your home? Did one of you own the house before you married or did you buy it jointly?

Length of Marriage – How long have you been married? Will you be seeking Alimony, or will your spouse? Do you even know if you are entitled to Alimony?

Communication with Spouse – Have you talked to your spouse about divorce or separation? Are you in agreement that a separation is imminent?

Financials – Can you afford to hire a divorce lawyer?

Adultery – Have either you or your spouse committed adultery?

These are just a few of the things to consider before deciding to hire a divorce lawyer. Generally, the decision regarding whether or not to hire a lawyer should be fairly easy.

You probably do not need a lawyer if all of the following apply:

- You have talked to your spouse and you both have decided to seek a separation and divorce

- You do not have any children

- You do not have any real property (i.e., you rent your home/apartment)

- You can divide up any assets you have without the assistance of a lawyer

- You cannot afford a lawyer, or would rather not spend your money hiring a lawyer

- Neither you nor your spouse have been unfaithful

- Neither you or your spouse require payment of Alimony

The above criteria most frequently describe a couple who decided to get married after a short courtship. Both husband and wife recognize that they made a bad decision and mutually decide to go their separate ways. This divorce is usually amicable, and the parties may stay friends afterward.

If this situation describes you, then you probably do not need a divorce lawyer. You may be a candidate for a number of "do-it-yourself" divorce services. You may need a lawyer if:

- You have talked to your spouse and both of you have agreed to a separation and divorce.

- You have minor children, and although you agree on the custody and visitation, you still need to calculate Child Support.

- You are intimidated by the courthouse and/or the thought of going in front of a judge by yourself.

- You are overwhelmed by the amount of paperwork that you must fill out to get a divorce.

- You are unsure of your legal rights and are afraid to proceed without consulting a lawyer.

- You are able to divide up all of your assets with your spouse, but you do not feel comfortable drafting a legal settlement agreement.

- You are willing to pay for a lawyer in return for the peace of mind that comes with not having to handle your divorce on your own.

- Your spouse hired a lawyer who has drawn up all the paperwork and you want someone to make sure it is legally correct.

If the above characteristics describe you, then you may want to consider hiring a lawyer. In all likelihood, if you have already divided up your assets and liabilities, and you are in agreement about who will be taking the kids, then you probably can proceed to handle the divorce on your own. However, if you are the type of person who feels overwhelmed by the legal system, or will forever second guess yourself for signing the documents your spouse's attorney prepared, then hiring a lawyer may not be such a bad idea.

In this situation, you could probably hire a lawyer to handle what is called an "uncontested divorce." If your divorce is truly "uncontested," most lawyers (myself included), will agree to draft all the paperwork necessary to complete your divorce, give you legal advice regarding the settlement you have reached, and even go to court with you to finalize your divorce after your one-year separation period. The best part? Most lawyers will do all this for a reduced fee, or possibly a flat fee. That means that you will pay one retainer, plus the costs for filing the case, and you do not need to worry about a lawyer billing your file on an hourly basis.

On the other hand, you should be prepared to hire an attorney if any of these factors apply:

- You have not talked to your spouse, or if you have, they do not agree to a separation or divorce.

- Your spouse left without so much as a goodbye (unfortunate, but it does happen).

- You have minor children, and you and your spouse have not agreed to custody or visitation, let alone Child Support.

- Your spouse is unwilling to pay Child Support.

- You are unable to divide shared assets and debts with your spouse.

- Either you or your spouse have committed adultery.

- You own a business or have a large amount of assets (some of which may be your separate property) that you want to protect.

- You are afraid you might have to pay Alimony.

- You feel you are entitled to receive Alimony.

- You are intimidated by the courthouse and/or the thought of going in front of a judge by yourself.

- You are overwhelmed by the amount of paperwork that you must fill out to get a divorce.

- You are unsure of your legal rights and are afraid to proceed without consulting a lawyer.

- Your spouse hired the most well-known and highly respected divorce lawyer in your area.

If the above characteristics describe your situation, you likely will want to hire a divorce lawyer to protect your rights. Even individuals with small salaries and very few assets will be impacted for years to come by the payment of Child Support or Alimony. Furthermore, you may be in a situation where a large amount of assets or debts must be divided. There may be tax implications involved when selling such assets. You will want to make sure that you are no longer on the hook for debts your spouse has incurred. For any of these reasons, it is a good idea to consult with a competent divorce lawyer.

In this situation, you will need to hire a lawyer. You will need to retain an attorney to handle what is called a "contested divorce." When you hire an attorney to handle this type of case, they will handle all aspects of your dissolution. They will negotiate with your spouse's attorney to attempt to settle the case during the post-separation period. They will schedule all court appearances and mediations. They will assist you in the preparation of your "discovery" materials. All in all, they will counsel you every step of the way to help you understand the legal process and make informed legal decisions.

CHAPTER SEVENTEEN

How to Hire the Right Divorce Lawyer

Before running out and hiring the first divorce lawyer you see online, in the yellow pages, on TV, or even one a friend referred you to, it is important to understand what hiring a lawyer means, and how lawyers work.

Divorce law is a highly specialized area of law. Many very specific rules and deadlines must be followed. Furthermore, a great deal of paperwork is involved in a divorce case. Hiring the wrong lawyer can prove to be a costly decision, not only in terms of lawyer fees, but in terms of the ultimate settlement that you can expect to receive at the conclusion of your case.

In this book, I have included useful information for anyone that is considering divorce, or who has already made that decision, but has not yet decided on which, if any, lawyer they want to hire.

14 QUESTIONS TO CONSIDER BEFORE HIRING A DIVORCE LAWYER

So you have finally scheduled a consultation with a lawyer. In all likelihood, you have never met with an attorney before, and you have no idea what to expect. Pay close attention early on in the interview, because how you are treated initially will be indicative of how you are treated as a client if you retain this lawyer.

Choosing a lawyer is a daunting task, and to make matters worse, you are expected to make this difficult decision while going through one of the most devastating emotional events of your life. You need a lawyer that you can trust completely, and with whom you will feel comfortable working with for as long as necessary (typically months, but possibly longer).

All lawyers are not created equal. Here are questions you should consider before handing over your credit card for the initial payment.

1. Is the lawyer's legal practice devoted entirely to family law and domestic relations?

We recommend that you choose a lawyer who practices primarily in the area of family and divorce law. This is a complicated and frequently changing area of the law. You need a lawyer in your corner who is experienced and knowledgeable in this practice area, not someone who merely dabbles in family law cases.

2. Does the lawyer pay attention to you while you are talking?

The initial consultation with your family lawyer is one of the most important meetings of your life. You need to ask yourself whether the lawyer cares about you and your case. You can tell a lot by how the lawyer treats you during the initial consultation. Do they pay attention to you and ask you specific questions about your case? Do they listen to what you are saying, or do they spend the meeting checking their phone or taking calls from other clients? The way the lawyer treats you during this initial meeting is a strong indication of how they will treat you as a client.

3. What is the lawyer's policy on returning phone calls promptly?

This is an extremely important question, and you should be wary of the response you receive. The best way an attorney will keep their client informed about the progress of their case is to first send them a copy of every piece of paper that goes in to or out of the law firm regarding case. The second way to keep clients informed is to pick up the phone.

The number one complaint about attorneys is that they do not return phone calls. Attorneys that do not return phone calls will have an equally difficult time keeping clients abreast of the activity in their case. Make sure that the lawyer you talk to has a written policy on how they keep their clients informed about the status of their case.

4. How selective is the lawyer in the cases they accept?

Does the lawyer you are considering accept every case that walks in their door or are they highly selective in the clients they choose to work with? Lawyers that accept any and all clients will have a hard time properly representing you because they will be too busy to give your case the attention it deserves. Make sure that your lawyer is selective in the cases they choose to accept.

5. Are you compatible with your lawyer?

It is important that you get along with and like your lawyer. You need to enjoy talking to them and spending time with them. You will get to know each very well in the coming months and need to be able to talk freely with them about some of the most intimate details of your life and finances. If you are not comfortable doing that with the lawyer you choose, it will hurt your case.

6. Does your lawyer have a plan of action?

You should hire a lawyer who is proactive in the way they handle their cases. They should have a clearly-mapped plan of attack for how they will approach your case and confidently convey this plan to you during your initial meeting.

7. Will the lawyer attempt to negotiate a settlement before filing a court action?

Many family lawyers default to immediately filing a lawsuit rather than attempting to negotiate a settlement. And for those lawyers who are willing to try negotiating, they take such a hardline position that they virtually guarantee your case will end up in court. Good lawyers understand that when it comes to family law cases, trials and hearings should be a last resort. They are expensive, take a great deal of time, and leave you with very little control over the outcome. There is certainly a time and place for taking a case to court, but all efforts to attempt a resolution out of court should be exhausted first.

8. Will your lawyer teach you about your case?

In a divorce situation, it is imperative that your lawyer be willing to communicate with you about your case, including educating you about how the law works and why certain settlement options are better than others. If you don't understand what is happening in your case, how can you expect to make decisions that could impact your life for years to come?

9. Is your lawyer confidently assertive without being arrogant?

Many people make the mistake of thinking they need to hire a strong-willed, arrogant "pit bull" type of attorney. However, this could be a huge mistake. In many cases, it is better to have a quiet yet confident attorney on your side. The arrogant and loud-mouthed attorney will quickly get a reputation in the community and may actually do you a disservice. There is no need to be obnoxious to be an effective advocate. Look for an attorney who is confident in their beliefs and thereby commands respect, rather than someone who squeezes every ounce of air out of a room.

10. What is your lawyer promising you?

You must be careful of any attorney that promises you the sun, moon, and stars at the initial consultation. No lawyer can guarantee any particular result. To do so is not only arrogant and stupid but also unethical. When you go to meet with a lawyer they know almost nothing about you (except what you tell them), nothing about your spouse, and will not typically know which attorney is representing your spouse or the judge involved in your case. The only thing your lawyer should guarantee to you is that they will do everything they can to advocate on your behalf. Anything more than that is merely a lie intended to convince you to retain them as your lawyer.

11. How will your lawyer keep you informed?

This is an extremely important question, and you should be wary of the response you receive. The best way an attorney will keep you informed about the progress of your case is to send you a copy of every piece of paper that comes into or out of their law firm for your case. Check to see if your client has an online client portal to share access to documents and information with their clients. An online client portal will provide you with immediate access to your entire client file, as well as notify you of important dates and actions taken in your case.

12. Who else will be working on your file?

It is important for you to understand who the primary attorney on your file will be. Sometimes the person who meets with you for the initial consultation is not the same attorney who will handle your case if you hire the firm. This is something you should know before you retain an attorney. In most larger firms, the senior partner you meet with will not be the person who ultimately handles your file on a day-to-day basis. That task will be delegated to a junior level associate or a paralegal. However, at smaller firms or with a solo practitioner, the attorney with whom you speak may very well be the person who is also taking care of your file. But be wary—even with some solo practitioners, a paralegal may be behind the scenes doing all the work on your file.

This is not always a bad thing. There are many very "menial" tasks that are just not worth the attorney's time to do. For example, organizing financial documents or drafting form motions does not always require the skills of a lawyer. And you certainly do not want that lawyer billing you $325 an hour or more to draft a form pleading. Better to save the attorney hours for the large amount of billable time spent preparing for and attending to hearings, mediation, and possibly trial.

13. How long will your divorce take?

It is important that you have a firm grasp on how long your case will take. A lawyer that cannot answer this question, or one that hems and haws at the question, may not know the answer. Obviously, nobody knows exactly how long a case will take to conclude. There are too many unknowns during an initial consultation, including who the opposing counsel is, how your spouse will act, how crowded the court docket is, which mediator will you use, etc.

Working with a difficult attorney will prolong a case. Being a difficult client will prolong a case. Choosing the wrong mediator will prolong a case. You just cannot say, at the very beginning, how long a case will take. But the lawyer should be able to give you a ballpark range based on their past experience in the county in which you live.

14. Why does the lawyer handle divorce cases?

How a lawyer answers this question will give you a great deal of insight into the type of attorney you are talking to and what their philosophies are about handling divorce cases. At The Hart Law Firm, we handle divorce cases because it gives us an opportunity to help someone who is going through one of the most difficult times of their life.

We believe that a divorce lawyer is different than all other types of lawyers. We do not just review contracts or represent faceless corporations. We represent real people with real problems. The agreements that we help our clients reach will impact them for the rest of their lives. We have a very real ability to help entire families cope with difficult problems and strengthen relationships between parents and their children.

While our advice is mostly legal, we can also counsel our clients on practical and everyday matters. Although we are lawyers by trade, that means that we are also every bit as much a counselor to our clients as the psychologist they would ordinarily see about their problems.

Even though it will not directly impact your "legal" case, in many ways the way in which the lawyer you interview answers this question will tell you a lot about the way they will help you to resolve your case.

CHAPTER EIGHTEEN

Before You Call to Schedule a Consultation

You should be aware of several things before you call to schedule an initial consultation with a divorce lawyer.

Consultation Fees

Many attorneys will charge consultation fees for the time they spend with you. This is especially true for divorce lawyers. The reason a consultation fee is necessary is that some spouses in especially contentious divorces will go from lawyer to lawyer all around town in an effort to "conflict" the good lawyers out of their case. This means that if you believe that several lawyers are the best to handle your divorce, and you have a consultation with each of them, then that lawyer will be unable to *even talk to* your spouse, let alone be retained as their lawyer.

Another reason that lawyers charge a consultation fee is that their time is valuable. Many have very busy practices and must find a way to eliminate those potential clients who only want to take an hour of their time to get free legal advice. They do this by charging a consultation fee.

Consultation fees vary from attorney to attorney. Some charge a two-hour minimum at their hourly rate, while other only charge for an hour of time. Some attorneys do not charge consultation fees, or allow for a free half hour consultation and then charge for their time after that. It all depends. You will want to pay what you feel comfortable paying.

"Your First Conversation..."

When you first call a law office to schedule a consultation, 99% of the time you will not speak with an attorney. The reason you will not talk to an attorney coincides with the reason that attorneys charge consultation fees. The paralegal or secretary you talk to will ask you questions about your case to get a sense of whether or not the attorney will accept your case before they are willing to pass you through.

Be prepared to answer basic questions about your spouse, your employer, how much money you make, what assets are at issue, if you own or rent, whether you have children, if custody is an issue, if you are separated, and more. One big question they will ask is the name of your spouse. If the attorney has already had a consultation with your spouse, they will not meet with you because they have been "conflicted out" of the case and cannot represent you anyway.

I once had a situation where my secretary had taken calls from both spouses in a divorce. The first one that got in to see me ended up being my client and I was unable to meet with the other one. A lot of my referrals come to me from attorneys who are conflicted out of a case, so they must pass the client on.

Lawyers Are Busy!

Remember this—lawyers are very busy, and their work comes in cycles. You may call one firm and are unable to meet with a lawyer for two weeks, whereas if you call another lawyer they are available the next day. This does not mean that one lawyer is any better than the other. If you called in two weeks, the situation could be flipped. Perhaps the one attorney was in trial all week and had to postpone all appointments. As soon as their case settled, they have more time to meet with clients.

Be patient when looking to hire a lawyer. Do not make a split-second decision unless you really like the attorney you meet with. This is a decision that is likely to remain with you the rest of your life. You should also beware of any attorney that tries to pressure you into retaining them. I always tell clients to take as much time as they need when deciding to hire me. Sometimes I meet with clients more than once before they make a decision. I want them to be happy with me as their lawyer and confident they have made the right choice. That is another reason I provide the information in this book—so that you can be an informed consumer *before* you meet with an attorney.

How WE WILL Handle Your Divorce Case

It may surprise you to hear that we do not conduct an initial consultation as do many other attorneys. Instead, we perform what has come to be known as a divorce or marriage "Assessment." We consider your first meeting with your divorce lawyer to be one of the most important and valuable meetings that you will ever have with an attorney. During the initial Assessment, we will obtain additional, historical information about you, your spouse, the marriage, and your family in general. We will talk to you about the law in North Carolina and go over tips and strategies that you may be able to use immediately. We will discuss the various options you have to settle your case, from the most cost-effective methods to the most expensive methods. We will answer any and all questions you may have about your case. At the end of the Assessment, we will talk to you about whether you need an attorney to handle your case, whether we will agree to handle your case, and what the cost may be. We will also talk to you about our value-based approach to billing and how this approach is a huge benefit to you.

Assuming that we do decide to accept you as a client, we will provide you with a financial affidavit and a list of documents you will need to disclose under North Carolina law. If litigation becomes necessary, our firm practice is to not file any pleadings until all financial disclosures have been made to our office.

In addition, as a new client you will receive a separation agreement questionnaire to fill out that will assist us in drafting your initial separation agreement. Once you have returned this document to our office with your initial financial disclosures, we will work with you to draft either a short memorandum that addresses all major issues that must be resolved, or a full separation agreement to send to your spouse or their lawyer if they have retained one. One of our biggest tasks at the initial stages of the divorce process is to collect as much financial information about you and your spouse as we can. The more homework you can do ahead of time, the easier our job will be at the outset.

After going back and forth with your spouse or their attorney several times, it may become apparent that a preliminary settlement will not be possible. At that point, we may choose to employ other methods of alternative dispute resolution, and/or file court paperwork to initiate litigation. In cases where Post Separation Support is needed, we may elect to file court paperwork sooner than normal (if the other spouse or their attorney is uncooperative). Once litigation has been filed, we expect that your spouse will answer our pleadings and perhaps file a countersuit. We will respond to these documents and place calls to your spouse's attorney to determine whether an early resolution will be possible. If not, we will proceed to prepare your case for trial.

As part of this preparation, it may also become necessary to conduct additional "discovery" to uncover additional financial information from your spouse, their employer, banks or other financial institutions, etc. Preparing your case for trial is a lengthy process that may involve hiring expert witnesses (accountants, consultants, etc.) or a Guardian ad Litem, (if there are children involved), taking depositions of key witnesses or your spouse, conducting additional discovery, and requesting and conducting pre-trial hearings. At some point, we will send the Court a notice that your case is ready for trial. At this point, an additional trial retainer may be needed.

Soon thereafter, the Court will conduct a Pre-Trial or Scheduling and Discovery Conference. At that time, the trial will be scheduled. In the weeks that follow, we will (if we have not already) gather additional evidence, meet with key witnesses, and conclude final preparations, and conduct a family law trial.

Throughout the entire process, we pride ourselves on keeping our clients up to date and informed about the status of their case. Our clients receive access to an online client portal that contains every piece of correspondence that comes in or goes out of our office for their case. We submit monthly bills to our clients so they know what work has been done and how much money is left on their engagement (retainer) fees. Finally, we will return all phone calls promptly and answer whatever questions our clients have about the process and what they can expect going forward.

OUR SERVICES

At The Hart Law Firm, P.A., we pride ourselves in providing personal service and individual attention to all of our clients. If your case meets our criteria for acceptance, you can be assured that you will receive close, personal attention from our lawyers and staff. We will keep you advised as to all aspects and stages of your case and keep you fully informed of all developments. You can call on us at any time should you have any questions about your case or to ask if we can help in any other way.

I sincerely hope that this book serves as a helpful reference tool for understanding how to prepare for your divorce and hire a divorce lawyer. If you have additional questions or think that we might be able to help you with your case, please feel free to call our office at (919) 460-5422. You may also contact us at www.jameshartlaw.com/contact/. My assistant will be happy to gather additional information from you and schedule your Divorce Assessment. In addition, my website (www.JamesHartLaw.com) is packed with a tremendous amount of information and free resources for people who are considering divorce.

Thank you again for taking the time to read this book. We hope that you found the information it contains to be helpful as you prepare yourself for the next steps.

CHAPTER NINETEEN
Your Next Steps: Final Thoughts

"He who represents himself has a fool for a client"
Abraham Lincoln

Divorce is scary. When you stood in front of your family and friends on your wedding day and told your spouse "I do", you never believed that you would be thinking about a separation or divorce, much less considering whether you should hire a lawyer to help you through this process. But here you are.

Divorce is an emotionally charged process. There are many legal implications to signing a separation and property settlement agreement. You should not go through this alone. Some couples are able to keep a level head about the process and negotiate an amicable settlement without the help of lawyers, but many others are unable to manage this process on their own.

If you are presented with a separation agreement that was drafted by your spouse's lawyer, **do not sign it without first talking to your own lawyer**. This is not just any old contract. This is a legally binding document that could affect you, your family, and your financial well-being for many years to come.

This book is intended to provide you with an overview of the legal process in North Carolina if you are considering a legal separation or divorce. Hopefully I have done a good job of conveying that information. However, this book is by no means a substitute for talking to or hiring a divorce lawyer to help you with your family law case.

Abraham Lincoln got it right with the quote at the beginning of this chapter. Just because you think you can negotiate a settlement on your own while avoiding investing in a lawyer to help you doesn't mean you should. Oftentimes the money and time with your kids that you may (unknowingly) give up in such a negotiation will far outweigh the financial investment to seek and hire a good lawyer to assist you.

If you live in the Triangle and are considering a legal separation or divorce, you may visit my website at www.jameshartlaw.com to learn more about how we might be able to help you. You don't need to go through this alone. We look forward to helping you through this process.

Jim Hart

For More Information

For more information on how to hire The Hart Law Firm for your divorce case, please visit our website, www.jameshartlaw.com.

The Hart Law Firm, P.A.
1143-B Executive Circle
Cary, North Carolina 27511
(919) 460-5422